Superstition: A Very Short Introduction

VERY SHORT INTRODUCTIONS are for anyone wanting a stimulating and accessible way into a new subject. They are written by experts, and have been translated into more than 45 different languages.

The series began in 1995, and now covers a wide variety of topics in every discipline. The VSI library currently contains over 600 volumes—a Very Short Introduction to everything from Psychology and Philosophy of Science to American History and Relativity—and continues to grow in every subject area.

Very Short Introductions available now:

ABOLITIONISM Richard S. Newman
THE ABRAHAMIC RELIGIONS
    Charles L. Cohen
ACCOUNTING Christopher Nobes
ADAM SMITH Christopher J. Berry
ADOLESCENCE Peter K. Smith
ADVERTISING Winston Fletcher
AESTHETICS Bence Nanay
AFRICAN AMERICAN RELIGION
    Eddie S. Glaude Jr
AFRICAN HISTORY John Parker and
    Richard Rathbone
AFRICAN POLITICS Ian Taylor
AFRICAN RELIGIONS
    Jacob K. Olupona
AGEING Nancy A. Pachana
AGNOSTICISM Robin Le Poidevin
AGRICULTURE Paul Brassley and
    Richard Soffe
ALEXANDER THE GREAT
    Hugh Bowden
ALGEBRA Peter M. Higgins
AMERICAN CULTURAL
    HISTORY Eric Avila
AMERICAN FOREIGN RELATIONS
    Andrew Preston
AMERICAN HISTORY Paul S. Boyer
AMERICAN IMMIGRATION
    David A. Gerber
AMERICAN LEGAL HISTORY
    G. Edward White
AMERICAN NAVAL HISTORY
    Craig L. Symonds
AMERICAN POLITICAL
    HISTORY Donald Critchlow

AMERICAN POLITICAL PARTIES
    AND ELECTIONS L. Sandy Maisel
AMERICAN POLITICS
    Richard M. Valelly
THE AMERICAN PRESIDENCY
    Charles O. Jones
THE AMERICAN REVOLUTION
    Robert J. Allison
AMERICAN SLAVERY
    Heather Andrea Williams
THE AMERICAN WEST Stephen Aron
AMERICAN WOMEN'S HISTORY
    Susan Ware
ANAESTHESIA Aidan O'Donnell
ANALYTIC PHILOSOPHY
    Michael Beaney
ANARCHISM Colin Ward
ANCIENT ASSYRIA Karen Radner
ANCIENT EGYPT Ian Shaw
ANCIENT EGYPTIAN ART AND
    ARCHITECTURE Christina Riggs
ANCIENT GREECE Paul Cartledge
THE ANCIENT NEAR EAST
    Amanda H. Podany
ANCIENT PHILOSOPHY Julia Annas
ANCIENT WARFARE Harry Sidebottom
ANGELS David Albert Jones
ANGLICANISM Mark Chapman
THE ANGLO-SAXON AGE John Blair
ANIMAL BEHAVIOUR
    Tristram D. Wyatt
THE ANIMAL KINGDOM
    Peter Holland
ANIMAL RIGHTS David DeGrazia
THE ANTARCTIC Klaus Dodds

For more information visit our website

www.oup.com/vsi/

Stuart Vyse

SUPERSTITION

A Very Short Introduction

OXFORD
UNIVERSITY PRESS

OXFORD
UNIVERSITY PRESS

Great Clarendon Street, Oxford, OX2 6DP,
United Kingdom

Oxford University Press is a department of the University of Oxford.
It furthers the University's objective of excellence in research, scholarship,
and education by publishing worldwide. Oxford is a registered trade mark of
Oxford University Press in the UK and in certain other countries

First edition published in 2019

Impression: 1

Published in the United States of America by Oxford University Press
198 Madison Avenue, New York, NY 10016, United States of America

British Library Cataloguing in Publication Data
Data available

Library of Congress Control Number: 2019947059

ISBN 978-0-19-881925-7

Printed in Great Britain by
Ashford Colour Press Ltd, Gosport, Hampshire

To my parents,
Norma M. Vyse
Arthur F. Vyse (1926–2010)

Contents

Preface

When I was asked to write *Superstition: A Very Short Introduction*, I was both honoured by the invitation and a bit bewildered by the task before me. Superstition is an endlessly fascinating subject explored in many books and scholarly articles, but no previous book had attempted to cover the entire landscape. Each of the subject areas of the chapters that follow has inspired several good books, and the interested reader will find many of them listed in the Further reading section at the end of this one. But no previous book—short or long—has attempted to tell the story of superstition from beginning to end. So, this little project represented a substantial responsibility. It is difficult to take such an enormous topic and boil it down to a pocket-sized book, but the work was aided by the history of superstition, which takes many twists and turns but follows a coherent arc from the beginning of civilization to the present day. As the following pages reveal, much of what was true about superstition in ancient times remains true today.

Part of our fascination with superstition comes from the mystery and paradox that attend it. Merely by being embedded in a culture, we all learn a number of luck-enhancing rituals, but it is often unclear how these superstitions—many of which are quite elaborate—got started. Chapter 4 includes a catalogue of some of the most common superstitions and their origins.

The paradox of superstition is that so many believe. In a world where the fruits of science are all around us, why do people appear to put their faith in magical forces? Psychological scientists have spent considerable time trying to answer this question, and in Chapter 5, I summarize what they have found.

Finally, Chapter 6 looks to the future of superstition. Magical thinking is unlikely to disappear any time soon, and its influence on our commercial markets has only grown. In this final chapter, I consider superstition's potential effects on society in the coming decades.

Acknowledgements

I am deeply indebted to a number of colleagues who read drafts of the book and provided helpful comments, including Eric Adler, Joseph Alchermes, Simon Feldman, Yibing Huang, Dale B. Martin, and the anonymous reviewers. Special thanks to Frederick Paxton, who provided good counsel from the very beginning. I would also like to acknowledge the valued support and many indulgences of friends and family members, including Emily Vyse, Graham Vyse, Norma Vyse, Keith Vyse, Kayo Nonaka, Gabby Arenge, Lynn Callahan, Jeff Callahan, Langdon Hammer, Uta Gosmann, Gary Greenberg, Perry Susskind, Kevin Plummer, Gary Stoner, Alex Hybel, Jan Hybel, Lee Hisle, Julie Worthen, Robert Gay, Sherri Storms, Frederick Paxton, Sylvia Malizia, Ross Morin, Simon Feldman, Kim Stillwell, Michael Reder, David Jaffe, Rachel Boggia, Lindsay Crawford, Bill Campbell, Kira Goldenberg, and Rachel Dreyer. My literary agent Jessica Papin contributed essential guidance, and at Oxford, it was a delight to work with Andrea Keegan, Jenny Nugee, Edwin Pritchard, Dorothy McCarthy, and Kayalvizhi Ganesan.

List of illustrations

Superstition

Chapter 1
The origins of superstition

You avoid taking a seat in the thirteenth row of an aeroplane. Your uncle carries a lucky stone in his pocket every day. A friend whose house is on the market buries a plastic St Joseph figurine in the front lawn in the hope of a quick sale. Being superstitious is not the kind of thing people brag about, but if you look around, there is quite a bit of it out there. It may seem paradoxical and irrational that superstition should persist in our modern world, but persist it does. Indeed, despite our rapidly increasing understanding of the universe, nature, and disease, there is some evidence that superstitious belief is waxing rather than waning. Even the most educated among us are not immune to its pull.

The concept of superstition has been with us for millennia, and yet today it has no agreed-upon meaning. We tend to know it when we see it—as in the examples above. If it carries a single enduring connotation, it is one of disapproval. From almost the very beginning, it was not a compliment to call someone superstitious. Throughout its long history, superstition has been a transactional concept with no fixed meaning of its own except in contrast to some other, more accepted world-view. As governments and systems of belief have changed, so have the targets of the label. As a result, the history of superstition is largely the story of a word and the different ways it has been applied.

The origin of the concept is found in ancient Greece, at least as far back as the 4th century BCE, and for the next 2,000 years superstition stood in contrast to the religious practices recommended by the elites. The word has often been levelled at practices that, even today, we would consider magical or paranormal, and yet versions of most of these practices are still with us.

Magic, prophecy, and divination in the ancient world

In many ancient cultures, shamans, magi, sorcerers, and prophets offered fortune telling and other magical services to the public. As part of their work, some of these shamans would achieve a trance state by bloodletting, smoking tobacco, or eating hallucinatory mushrooms.

During the Shang Dynasty (c.1560–1050 BCE) and beyond, shamanic divination was conducted by members of the ruling family who were in touch with the spirits of the afterlife. The shaman would receive offerings of food and wine. Questions to be asked of spirits in the afterworld were carved into animal bones or turtle shells, which were heated until cracks appeared. Often the message was thought to have been carried by an animal spirit that rose to heaven to speak with ancestors and gods. The cracks in the heated object provided clues to what the future would bring and what action the supplicant should take.

The most famous of all methods of Chinese fortune telling is described in the *I Ching*, also known as the *Book of Changes*. Armed with a bundle of fifty sticks made from the dried stalks of a yarrow plant, the diviner used a random process to determine a hexagram combination of six broken or unbroken lines (see Figure 1). Each of the hexagrams had an accompanying commentary. The original versions of the *Book of Changes*, dating from the first millennium BCE, were written on bamboo strips that

1. The hexagram Chun, from the *I Ching* (Book of Changes).

were bound together into scrolls or books. The *I Ching* was used extensively for thousands of years in China, and continues to be studied today. The famous Swiss psychiatrist Carl Jung (1875–1961) was fascinated with the *I Ching* because he believed the manipulation of the yarrow sticks opened a window into the user's unconscious.

The archaic English word *mage* derives from the Old Persian word maguš, which is also the origin of the English word magic. In ancient Persia, mages were professional wise people who engaged in several forms of divination, including dream interpretation, astrology, augury (reading patterns in the flights of birds), and necromancy (communicating with or raising the dead). In the Greek writer Aeschylus' 5th-century-BCE play *The Persians*, a chorus of Persian elders calls up the ghost of Darius, who is the father of the current king, Xerxes. Darius appears, expresses his disappointment with the hubris of his son, and offers the prophecy that Xerxes will be defeated in battle, a prediction that is later fulfilled.

Magic in ancient Egypt was well integrated into government and religion. Rather than being independent magicians or shamans, most ancient Egyptian magicians were members of the priesthood. Cultic temples to the gods were staffed by local priests who often engaged in magic. The magical texts that have survived from Egypt suggest that priest-magicians offered spells that often enlisted the help of the gods. One of the most notable of Egyptian practitioners was Prince Khaemwaset, the fourth son

3

of Ramses II (1279–1213 BCE) and Queen Isetnofret. Khaemwaset was a famous priest and collector of magical items, including many powerful amulets. He also maintained a library of spell books.

Greek mythology and history is filled with prophets, oracles, and seers who possessed a variety of dazzling powers. In Sophocles' tragedy *Oedipus Rex*, the blind prophet Tiresias reveals that Oedipus has murdered the former king of Thebes, a suggestion that Oedipus initially rejects, ridiculing Tiresias as a beggar-priest and a charlatan motivated only by money. Later Oedipus discovers that the blind prophet was right and that, furthermore, Laius, the former king of Thebes, was his father.

According to a number of authors, the 6th-century-BCE Greek philosopher Pythagoras, discoverer of the Pythagorean Theorem, had several supernatural abilities. Like seers in a number of cultures, Pythagoras was reported to have descended into the underworld, returning with special wisdom. He also demonstrated the skill of bilocation: appearing in two different cities on the same day and time. Finally, Pythagoras was purported to have remarkable control over natural events: predicting earthquakes and quelling pestilences, hailstorms, and rough seas.

In the *Republic*, Plato portrays beggar-priests as immoral vendors who presented themselves to the rich, looking for money. When their customers had committed injustices, these itinerant prophets offered to repair the situation with sacrifices and incantations. Even worse (in Plato's view), when the wealthy were troubled by some enemy or rival, the priests readily offered to harm the offending party with spells and curses—whether these punishments were justified or not.

Many ancient shamans, sorcerers, and magicians claimed to have special abilities for treating diseases, sometimes putting themselves in competition with established physicians.

The papyrus manuscripts that survive suggest that the Egyptians had acquired considerable medical knowledge. Although they conducted only a few surgical procedures, they had developed methods of removing bone fragments and dressing wounds, and they employed many specialized poultices and medicines, which frequently contained blood or excrement. But the priests and physicians who treated medical problems also performed spells and incantations. Some priests were part-time scorpion charmers who claimed to have power over the scorpion god and the ability to protect patients against the bites of scorpions and snakes. Sometimes a spell would accompany a more practical treatment. For example, honey was often applied to burns and wounds, and its use was often combined with a 'spell for the honey' aimed at preventing infection. Magical techniques were particularly common when a more practical treatment was not available. For example, the standard methods of setting a bone did not involve magical procedures, but the treatment of headache did.

In Greece, a work credited to the great physician Hippocrates (c.460–370 BCE), but probably not written by him, contains a scathing attack on beggar-priests, calling them charlatans who falsely claimed to have influence over the gods. Rather than approaching the gods in the traditional pious ways, such as visiting temples, making offerings, and praying, beggar-priests made the preposterous (to the Hippocratic author) claim that diseases were the work of various gods, and that they, the priests, had influence over the gods. In contrast, the Hippocratic author argued that no particular god would directly infect any individual person with disease and that the truly pious Greek would not attempt to move the gods—except through the traditional methods of expressing devotion. Of course, the line between established medical practice and that of the beggar-priests was often difficult to see, and as a result, the Hippocratic criticisms can be seen as part of an ancient turf war among professionals.

In general, Greek and Roman authors had a low regard for magic and its purveyors. Often magic was portrayed as a kind of foreign invasion, brought into society by alien visitors. The 1st-century-CE Roman author Pliny the Elder expressed the view that magic had originated with ancient Zoroastrians in Persia. Similarly, in the Greek and Roman worlds, Egypt was seen as a particularly fertile source of magic. The Egyptians' use of papyrus and their elaborate processes of mummification and burial looked exotic and mysterious to the Greeks, suggesting that Egyptians had access to esoteric forms of knowledge. As the term beggar-priests suggests, sorcerers and shamans were often associated with the lower classes, and Plutarch, among others, ridiculed these shamans, pointing to the obvious contradiction of their circumstances. If they were able to bring good fortune, why were they so poor?

Curses and binding spells

In addition to magic that required a professional intermediary, people in the ancient world often engaged in their own private forms of supernatural practice. Because curses and binding spells involved a variety of materials that have survived the intervening millennia, we know quite a bit about how these methods were applied. The earliest known use of binding spells—curses aimed at binding or restricting the actions of a targeted individual—is in the 6th century BCE, and the practice continued into the early centuries CE.

The most common medium for the binding spells that have survived is tablets made of lead (see Figure 2). Lead was pliable, inexpensive, and could easily be rolled out into a thin sheet that was a good writing surface. The spell would be etched into the lead with a bronze stylus—often on both sides of the sheet—after which the tablet was typically rolled up and pierced with nails. Many of the tablets seem to be the work of professional scribes or magicians, others are more likely the work of amateurs.

2. Curse tablet found in London.

Sometimes binding curses involved a form of sympathetic magic, similar to voodoo, that required a figurine in human shape, most likely the work of a professional magician. These figures were constructed out of clay, brass, or wax and they often depicted the target of the curse with their arms bound behind them. A clay figure at the Louvre Museum in Paris shows a woman who has been pierced by a number of copper needles (see Figure 3). The figure was found inside a clay pot along with a lead curse tablet containing a love curse written in Greek. Like many love curses, the goal was to have the person depicted by the figurine develop or maintain desire for the person commissioning the curse. Although these figurines were often pierced with needles, the purpose was not to kill or injure the object of the charm. According to the spell instructions found on Egyptian papyri, an incantation was spoken as each needle was inserted: 'I pierce the stomach of X, that she may think of no one but me.'

3. A clay figurine used in a binding curse.

Because burial grounds were a kind of gateway to the underworld, curse tablets and binding curse figurines were often placed in graves or caskets. The messages written on the tablets often appealed to gods (usually Hermes or Persephone), demons, or ancestors to perform the desired actions. Most often the goal of a binding spell was to harm someone without killing them, and there were a variety of situations that might provoke an Egyptian, Greek, or Roman to employ this tactic. Among the most common uses were to: attack a commercial rival in order to succeed in the marketplace; inhibit the performance of an athlete or other public figure; achieve a romantic conquest by instigating a separation (freeing up the intended lover) or stimulating affection for the user; or ensure a desired outcome in legal proceedings.

One of the surviving tablets was designed to bind the limbs of two runners so that 'they be neither powerful nor strong'. The tablet also invoked demons to keep the competitors up all night and prevent them from eating before the race. In addition to cursing the opponents of favoured athletes, in Greece it was not uncommon to curse an actor in a theatrical competition so that a preferred competitor might prevail.

The romantically motivated curses often suggested a love triangle, with the person commissioning the curse hoping to break up a couple so that the object of affection might be free to come to them. One Greek tablet of the 3rd or 2nd century BCE was buried with the body of someone named Theonnastos and was designed to sabotage the rival Zoilos and attract the attention of Antheira. It was a very long-winded curse, but it included the following, rather nasty line: 'Just as you, Theonnastos are powerless in the movement of your hands, your feet, your body…so too may Zoilos be powerless to come to Antheira, and Antheira be powerless to come to Zoilos.' Other curses beseeched a god or other intermediary to prevent an intended lover from loving or having intercourse with anyone other than the commissioner of the curse.

The largest category of Greek curse tablets appears to have been aimed at winning in court proceedings. In Athens, citizens were required to appear in court to plead their case. Generally, these judicial curse tablets were written before the outcome of the trial, and they often invoked Hermes or another god to intervene and make the opponent or the opponent's advocate inarticulate in court. If someone who was known to be an effective orator performed poorly in court, it was commonly assumed that they had been the victim of a curse.

One of the most interesting examples of the use of curse tablets came with the discovery of 130 of them at the Temple to Sulis-Minerva at Bath, England. During much of the first four centuries CE, the southern half of Britain was part of the Roman Empire, including the area that is now London. There is a thermal spring at Bath, and long before the Roman conquest, Britons erected a temple to the Celtic god Sulis and established a public bath at the spring. The Romans later associated Sulis with their god Minerva, and the baths remained in operation for centuries.

Analysis of the Bath curse tablets reveals that they are written in Latin and almost all of them appear to have been aimed at punishing thieves. A common problem when visiting baths—throughout the ancient world, not just in Bath—was theft of clothes and other possessions. The bather would emerge from the water naked, only to find that their belongings had disappeared in their absence. This must have been a very frustrating experience, and it appears that, at Bath, a cottage industry of curse tablet vendors stood ready to capitalize on the bathers' anger. One of the more vicious Bath curses inspired by a stolen silver ring was translated as follows:

> Basilia gives (in) to the temple of Mars (her) silver ring so long as (someone), whether slave or free, keeps silent or knows anything about it, he may be accursed in (his) blood and eyes and every limb, or even have all (his) intestines quite eaten away, if he has stolen the ring or been privy to (the theft).

Before we leave the topic of curse tablets and binding spells, it is worth noting that many of the binding curses in the ancient world employed a form of sympathetic magic identified by the Scottish anthropologist Sir James George Frazer in his famous multivolume book *The Golden Bough* (1890). Frazer described two principles of sympathetic magic: similarity and contagion. Contagion was the belief that objects that were once in contact continue to have a lasting connection after separation. For example, some curses employ the victim's blood, hair, or nail clippings in the construction of a poppet, doll, or effigy in an effort to employ contagious magic.

Similarity is the idea that things that look similar have a connection. When binding curses employed figurines, they were designed to look like the target individual in an effort to capitalize on this principle. In addition, curses written on sheets of lead often drew a similarity between the tablet itself (or other aspects of the spell) and the desired action. We have already seen a case of this in the romantically motivated curse that compared the dead body near which it was placed with the intended effect. Other curses made reference to the lead itself. For example, 'Just as lead is cold and useless, so may _____ be cold and useless.'

These principles of sympathetic magic will make many appearances throughout the history of superstition and continue to be important today.

Superstition as excessive piety

Given all the myth, fortune telling, and magic in the ancient world, you might assume the concept of superstition began by labelling some religious or magical practices out of bounds. Accepted forms of religious worship—even those activities that today we consider superstitious—might have become endorsed forms of piety and others not.

Rather surprisingly, that's not how the idea got started. Although, as we have seen, much of the magic of the ancient world was considered unorthodox and dangerous, the earliest concept of a superstition did not start here. It began as a dismissive term for a certain kind of religious worship.

The word superstition took many turns before arriving at the meaning we give it today. It derives from the Latin *superstitio*, which is made from the roots *stare*, 'to stand', and *super*, 'over'. Together they mean to 'stand over', and the word is sometimes interpreted as standing over something in awe. The implication is that too much power or reverence has been given to something undeserving, but we are getting a little ahead of ourselves. The concept of superstition began as the Greek word *deisidaimonia* (δεισιδαιμονία), which in the 4th century BCE had the positive meaning 'scrupulous in religious matters'; but a century later it had acquired a more negative meaning, inching it closer to our modern understanding of superstition. The philosopher Theophrastus (371–287 BCE) wrote a book containing thirty brief character sketches of the types of men commonly encountered on the streets of Athens—some of which were humorous and all of which were unflattering. Number sixteen was 'The Superstitious Man', who exhibited 'cowardice with regard to the divine'.

> The Superstitious Man is the kind who washes his hands in three springs, sprinkles himself with water from a temple font, puts a laurel sprig in his mouth, and then is ready for the day's perambulations.

It is not so much that the rituals and beliefs of the Superstitious Man were considered false or inappropriate or foreign but that they were excessive and lacking moderation. Furthermore, the rituals of the superstitious person were assumed to stem from a misplaced fear of the gods. Based on this early meaning of *deisidaimonia*, it is easy to see how it was translated into Latin as *superstitio*, excessive awe or fear of the gods. Three centuries later the Greek biographer Plutarch (*c*.46–120 CE) wrote an essay 'On Superstition', in which he argued that the superstitious person was worse than an atheist because 'The atheist thinks there are no gods; the superstitious man wishes there were none, but believes in them against his will; for he is afraid not to believe.' The establishment view was that the gods were real and had pervasive influence on everyday life, but they were generally benevolent and need not be feared. Plutarch argued that although atheists were frequently accused of impiety, the superstitious person was even more at fault.

These ideas about correct and incorrect understanding of the gods and worship were reinforced by the accepted views of medicine and social structure in the Greek classical period (479–323 BCE). Hippocrates separated himself from many Greeks of that era who believed illness was willed by the gods. In his essay *On the Sacred Disease* Hippocrates criticized 'witch-doctors, faith-healers, quacks and charlatans' who claimed epilepsy was caused by a kind of personalized 'divine vengeance', and offered purification rituals—some involving washing with the blood of sacrificed animals—and other spells they said would placate the gods and cure the ailment. Hippocrates believed there was divinity in disease, just as there was divinity in all things, but the influence of the gods was more distant and benevolent than suggested by these healers. He rejected the idea that the gods were temperamentally capable of causing illness. 'Personally, I believe human bodies cannot be polluted by a god; the basest object by the most pure.'

The Greek philosophers Socrates (as reported by Plato) and Aristotle further cemented the notion that fear of the gods did not make sense and, as a result, sacrifices and purification rituals were not necessary. Socrates asserted that if the gods were supremely blessed, it stood to reason that they were also supremely virtuous. Happiness could not be obtained without virtue, and thus the gods must have both qualities. As a result, their virtuous nature would not allow them to intentionally bring harm, which meant there was no reason to fear them. Aristotle further supported these ideas with a teleological view of nature, suggesting that things were as they were because it was the best possible solution given the constraints. For example, although some writers believed human hands were a sign of human intelligence, Aristotle argued that humans were given hands because they were intelligent. Humans and animals were designed as they were because they represented the best possible arrangement. To believe otherwise would be superstitious. Finally, both men supported a hierarchical view of the cosmos with gods and heroes at the top, humans below, and animals below that. This sense of hierarchy carried over into an implicit system of social status with the philosophers who eschewed *deisidaimonia* on top and the common people who engaged in fearful superstitious rituals below. Although there are many counterexamples and the common stereotype is not entirely true, even today superstition is stereotypically associated with the less-educated classes.

Superstition as belief in foreign cults

This still only gets us part of the way to our present meaning of superstition. The next step was taken with the translation of *deisidaimonia* into Latin as *superstitio*, the root of our modern English word. Initially *superstitio* retained the meaning of fearful religiosity. *Superstitio* was excessive *religio* (religion). For example, in the mid-1st century BCE, the Roman statesman Cicero (106–43 BCE) used the term to describe 'Those who spent whole days in prayer and offered sacrifices that their children might outlive them.' Elsewhere he wrote that superstition 'implied a groundless fear of the gods'; whereas religion 'consists in piously worshipping them'. Like the Greeks, Roman philosophers looked down on superstition because it represented a surrender to fear and passion, which were considered antithetical to the goals of society. Furthermore, the endorsement of evil forces inherent to superstition conflicted with the ordered sense of the universe promoted by the elites.

But by the 1st century CE, a change in the meaning of *superstitio* started to take hold. The practice of superstition acquired an additional sense of being anti-Roman. The label *superstitio* was often applied to the religions of the peoples the Romans had conquered—particularly when the continued practice of these non-Roman religions was judged to be a threat. As we have seen, the Greeks also believed that the magic and religion of foreign places was dark and suspicious, but it was not until the 1st century

14

CE that the *superstitio* label was used to describe something that was in opposition to the state. Particularly among the elite, *superstitio* described the mysterious and distasteful religions of other peoples.

Once it had acquired the pejorative meaning of alien religion, it was not long before the charge of superstition was levelled against the young sect of Christianity. For example, the Roman senator and historian Tacitus (*c*. 56–120 CE) described Christianity as a 'recurrent superstition' that was spreading from Judaea. Furthermore, the history of the Christians strengthened the view that they were a threat to Roman rule. Rather than following the emperor, they worshipped a Jew, known as 'The King of the Jews', who had been executed for treason by the Romans.

This transformation of the Latin *superstitio* was the first clear instance of superstition taking on the meaning of 'bad religion'—not just excessive religion—that it would retain for many centuries. In the following years, the religions labelled superstitious or non-superstitious would alternate several times, but until the period we call the Enlightenment, superstition's primary target was the religion of competing groups.

Chapter 2
Religious superstition

For more than three centuries of the common era the traditional Graeco-Roman panoply of gods remained the official religion of the state. Cultic shrines were constructed throughout the Empire, and the traditional feast days and established demonstrations of piety continued. The word *superstitio* had acquired its new sense of anti-state subversion, and although the epithet was aimed at a variety of targets—particularly foreign forms of worship and magic or competing methods of divination—Roman authors soon took aim at the upstart religion invading from Judaea.

Before Christianity began to emerge as a force in the Mediterranean region, official Judaism derided what it considered to be the pagan religions of the Canaanites. Chapter 18 verses 9–11 of the Book of Deuteronomy from the Hebrew Bible, which is thought to have been written in Israel of the 7th century BCE, states: 'you must not learn to imitate the abhorrent practices of those nations. No one shall be found among you who makes a son or daughter pass through fire (in human sacrifice), or who practises divination, or is a soothsayer, or an augur, or a sorcerer, nor one who casts spells, or who consults ghosts or spirits, or who seeks oracles from the dead.' In addition, the worship of a single god made it easier to draw a contrast between Jewish belief and those of their polytheistic neighbours.

The Greeks associated the East with magic, and, despite the biblical injunctions against the abhorrent practices of other nations, Jews were very strongly associated with magic. They were considered skilful at exorcism, and they often offered amulets for the cure of diseases. For example, a small gold amulet found near Beirut, Lebanon, and thought to date from between the 1st century BCE and the 1st century CE, contained an incantation written on gold foil that was aimed at curing a woman's 'wandering womb', a Greek medical theory that gave rise to the concept of hysteria and was blamed for a variety of physical and psychological conditions. According to common Greek and Roman stereotype, Jews were steeped in magic and more successful magicians than other purveyors.

It appears that Christians did not immediately come to the attention of Romans. The Emperor Claudius expelled all the Jews from Rome in the middle of the 1st century CE for too aggressively proselytizing in the city, but there is some evidence that, at that time, Romans did not distinguish between Jews and followers of Christ. By the beginning of the 2nd century, however, this new religion was viewed with greater suspicion. Although the three wise men of the nativity story were cast as Persian magi and astrologers who became the first converts from old magical beliefs to Christianity, Jesus of Nazareth's own performance of miracles would soon lead to accusations that he was an eastern magician. In the 2nd century CE, the philosopher Celsus claimed that the young Jesus had travelled to Egypt to study magic in the land best known for sorcery and occult knowledge. Furthermore, as an itinerant beggar, Jesus fitted the classic image of a vagabond priest and magician. Christians competed with local magicians for adherents, and the Roman writers of the early Christian period were critical of this new sect. By the end of the 1st century CE, Christianity became the most reviled of the anti-Roman faiths.

In 112 CE Pliny the Younger, who at the time was serving as governor in a northern section of modern Turkey, wrote to

Emperor Trajan (r. 98–117 CE) about the local Christians he had encountered. Pliny's research revealed that Christians met before dawn to sing hymns to their god, and that they took oaths not to steal, lie, or commit adultery. He found nothing particularly harmful in their actions, which he described as merely a 'depraved immoderate *superstitio*'. Nonetheless, Pliny believed that the Christians' refusal to make sacrifices to the gods or the emperor when asked to do so was sufficient reason to punish them with death.

During this early period in the history of their religion, Christians were blamed for things that went wrong. The historian Tacitus likened Christians to a disease that had spread from Judaea to Rome and reported that the Emperor Nero (r. 54–68 CE) blamed them for a devastating fire in Rome. Thus, according to some members of the Roman elite, Christianity was a foreign scourge that should be curtailed. The biographer Suetonius wrote a document listing all of Nero's accomplishments in improving Roman civic life, including establishing limits on excesses, such as discouraging lavish banquets and forbidding the sale of luxurious delicacies at roadside taverns. In addition, Suetonius noted that Nero had punished the Christians, who were 'in the grip of a new and maleficent *superstitio*'.

Superstition as pagan belief

Throughout the early centuries of the common era, Christianity continued to gain popularity, putting the government in Rome in an awkward position. The turning point came in 313, when Emperor Constantine prohibited the persecution of Christians and other minority religious groups and promoted Christianity in Rome. Despite traditional Roman polytheism being the most popular religion for some years to come, Constantine outlawed blood sacrifices—which Christians found particularly abhorrent—and converted on his deathbed, becoming the first Christian emperor. During his brief reign Emperor Julian

(r. 361–3) attempted to re-establish traditional Roman religion and limit the practice of Christianity, but this effort ultimately failed. Under Theodosius I (r. 379–95) Christianity became the official religion, and the leadership of the Roman Empire would be Christian from that point forward. The once proud tradition of Roman ancestors and cultic worship of the gods was labelled a pagan religion. Similarly, the word *superstitio* reversed course and was now used against those who once used it against Christians.

Celsus v. Origen and Firmicus v. Firmicus

The changing view of superstition that ultimately produced the switch of Roman religion from traditional polytheism to Christianity is revealed in a dialogue between Celsus and Origen. As we have seen, Celsus was a strongly anti-Christian writer whose defence of traditional religion was grounded in the philosophers. In much the way Greek and Roman philosophers had called people of the lower classes superstitious when they exhibited an exaggerated fear of demons (*deisidaimonia*), Celsus rejected the Christian form of demonology. Christians believed in the existence of devils who performed evil acts. Celsus, like the philosophers, maintained that, because they were superior to humans, demons could only do good. Celsus viciously attacked Christian beliefs because they violated what the philosophers believed to be the natural hierarchy. Why would a god submit to incarnation in the body of a lowly Jew? In addition, Celsus described Christians as poor, despicable, and superstitious.

Origen Adamantius (*c*.184–253 CE) was a prolific Christian writer, educated in Alexandria, who made a direct response in a work called *Contra Celsum* (Against Celsus), written in 248 CE. Origen sidestepped some of Celsus's points by suggesting he had confused 'true Christians' with 'heretics' or with Jews, of whom Origen was also critical. Celsus had criticized Christianity for being a new religion whose god does not protect adherents from oppression and torture, but Origen replied that the rapid growth of Christianity must be a sign of divine approval. Finally, Celsus had belittled Jesus for his poverty and his willing acceptance of his crucifixion, but Origen cleverly pointed out that the same could be said of Socrates and that many of the Greek philosophers were also poor.

The movement from paganism to Christianity was a gradual process in the early decades of the 4th century, and there is an interesting example of this transition within the writings of a single person. Firmicus Maternus was a member of the Roman senatorial class who wrote the *Mathesis*, a long and famous text on Roman astrology. At the time he wrote the *Mathesis* in the years 337–40 CE, Firmicus was a believer in the traditional Roman gods, and he used the word *superstitio* in its classical sense of the overly fearful nature of some pagan rituals. But later he converted to Christianity, and in a polemical work, *De Errore Profanarum Religionum* written in 346, he urged Constantine's sons, who had succeeded Constantine I, to stamp out *superstitio*, in this case, meaning pagan religious practices.

Superstition as common magic

As Christianity began to solidify its power in the 4th and 5th centuries, a number of theologians emerged to create important works of doctrine, some of which took on the task of separating accepted religious practices from magic and superstition. One of these was Augustine of Hippo (354–430), a north African who would become an important saint. Augustine was educated in Carthage and was drawn to philosophy and Manichaeism before converting to Christianity and eventually rising to the position of Bishop of Hippo Regius, now the city of Annaba, Algeria. Like a number of writers before him, Augustine attacked superstition on two different fronts: he made the kind of class-based criticisms we associate with Greek and Roman philosophers, as well as the Christian anti-pagan attacks typical of the Roman Christian establishment. In addition, Augustine is particularly important for our purposes because he addressed, not just the magic and ritual of discredited pagan religions, but the more common household luck-enhancing practices we recognize as superstitions today.

In a work called *De Doctrina Christiana* (On Christian Teaching), Augustine called all forms of magic superstitious because they required some kind of involvement with demons—a theme that would be repeated for centuries, particularly in the age of witchcraft. He denounced spells, incantations, and divination, including astrology. In the medical realm, Augustine aimed his criticism at the popular use of protective or curative amulets, taking a position that was similar to classical Roman physicians. When it came to more common superstitions, Augustine showed a kind of derision of believers that was similar to ancient Greek and Roman philosophers and reminiscent of the original meaning of *deisidaimonia*.

In *The City of God* (written between 413 and 426), Augustine made his most definitive case against superstition and magic. Although the Eastern Empire would survive for more than 1,000 years, by the 5th century, a number of conflicts with the Germanic peoples of the north eventually led to the demise of the Western Empire. One such conflict was the sacking of Rome in 410 by the Visigoths, and as an explanation for this setback, supporters of the traditional pagan religion claimed that Rome had been weakened by 'Christian superstition'. Augustine argued against this view in *City of God* and asserted that the true source of superstition was in the traditional Roman cults, not Christianity. He likened Roman worship to common magicians who relied on demons for their power. In contrast, Christians achieved their ends by praying to the Christian god who responded with miracles.

In subsequent years, despite the decline of the Empire in the west, Christianity continued to spread north and west, gradually overtaking the various pagan religions of Germans, Celts, Iberians, and other groups. Thus, just as the Roman Empire was losing its central control over much of the Mediterranean region, the Roman church was becoming disentangled from any particular nation and more centralized in Rome. As part of an effort to maintain authority, Christian doctrine became more formalized. For example, in the 6th century, church councils produced handbooks for penances, known as penitentials, that outlined the kinds of penances required for various infractions. Among other things, these documents make clear that people who engaged in superstitions were required to repent and make amends. In general, the consequences were relatively mild, such as fasting for a period of time or engaging in some devotional activity, but when the magic or superstition was employed for malicious purposes, the penance was more severe.

Superstitio continued to morph into various meanings as local needs demanded, as shown in the *indiculi superstitionum* that began to appear in the 6th and 7th centuries. One surviving example is the *indiculus superstitionum et paganiarum* (small list of superstitions and paganisms), preserved in the *Codex Palatinus Latinus 577*, a church document that probably originates from the mid-to-late 8th century in a Frankish or Germanic area of northern Europe. This particular *indiculus* lists thirty different prohibitions; however, they are only briefly described without any introduction or additional explanation. Among the forbidden activities are examples of common superstitions and vestiges of Roman religion, as well as activities that were Christian in origin but considered heretical or containing pagan or superstitious elements. The more common superstitious prohibitions included incantations (*indiculus* 12) and a variety of divinatory activities, such as augury by the observation of birds or horses or the examination of cattle dung (*indiculus* 13). Traditional pagan influence is evident in prohibitions against feasts in February (3) or in honour of Mercury and Jupiter (8), which may have also applied to equivalent gods from the Germanic pantheon (Wotan and Donar). There are also admonitions against sacrifices at the graves of the dead (2) and worshipping at cultic temples (4).

Interestingly, this list also includes a number of practices that may reflect the ragged edges of superstition or paganism blending with Christianity. For example, the *indiculus* prohibited sacrifices made to the saints (9), worshipping of saints in inappropriate places (18), and seeking what belongs to St Mary (it is not entirely clear what this meant) (19). Mixtures like these probably proceeded in two directions. We know that some Christians incorporated pagan practices into their worship, and it is also quite likely that some pagans adopted features of Christianity. The admonitions of the *indiculus superstitionum et paganiarum* were aimed at a number of goals, and they do not tell us how common these practices were. But it is clear the church hierarchy was concerned about the items on this list and felt it important to draw lines separating accepted Christian worship from pagan, superstitious, or heretical acts.

In the last centuries of the first millennium CE, the attacks on magic and superstition in central Europe became much more aggressive. After the fall of the Western Roman Empire, the power of the Franks grew steadily until under Charlemagne (742–814) it encompassed modern-day Germany, Belgium, the Netherlands, France, and northern Italy. Charlemagne became king and, eventually, emperor, and during his rule, imperial and religious power were once again united in a particularly powerful combination. For example, after a series of wars that eventually defeated the Germanic people of Saxony, Charlemagne issued a decree requiring that any Saxon who refused conversion to Christianity be put to death. Throughout his reign Charlemagne produced a number of edicts against superstition, magic, and pagan religious practices. In 789 he issued the *Admonitio Generalis* (General Admonition) that applied throughout his kingdom and outlawed all forms of divination and magical practices. Working magicians and sorcerers were forced to renounce their practices or face death. In 800 a church synod at Freising instructed bishops to investigate any reports of divination, incantations, or weather magic, and they were authorized to use torture in their investigations if needed.

Weather magic appears to have been a particular concern in the early 9th century. Around 820, Archbishop Agobard of Lyon described popular panics caused by the belief that crops had been destroyed by the magical production of hailstorms and other weather phenomena. These fears led to frequent lynchings of suspected weather magicians (*tempestarii*). But suspicions about weather magic were not the only concerns in the 9th century. A church synod at Pavia in 850 reported that magic and superstition were still a substantial problem, particularly love spells and magic used to injure or kill. A famous case of love spells involved King Lothar II, a great-grandson of Charlemagne. Lothar had married Theutberga, but because she proved to be incapable of bearing children, Lothar sought a divorce so that he could wed his mistress, Waldrada. As a first attempt, Lothar charged his wife with a particularly offensive form of adultery—incest with her brother—and attempted to make his case using a test that, although accepted at the time, looks very brutal to modern observers. The nobility of the era were allowed to divorce if sufficient grounds could be found, and if a wife was discovered to have been unfaithful, it was not unusual for her husband to kill her. In order to test for adultery, Theutberga was subjected to a boiling water ordeal, however, being a queen, she was able to assign a substitute to take the test. The procedure involved retrieving an object from the bottom of a cauldron filled with boiling water, after which the injured hand was bandaged. If, when the bandages were removed three or four days later, the hand was deemed to be 'uncooked'—which presumably meant healing normally—then the test was passed. Theutberga's substitute emerged 'uncooked', and Theutberga was judged innocent. Lothar would have to find another way to get a divorce.

The saga of Lothar, Theutberga, and Waldrada would go back and forth for years and end unresolved in 869 when Lothar fell ill and died at the age of 34. Archbishop Hincmar of Rheims, who was both a historian of the events and a participant who very much opposed the divorce of Lothar and Theutberga, wrote an account of the controversy, *De Divortio Lotharii Regis e Teutbergae Reginae* (On the Divorce of King Lothar and Queen Theutberga). Hincmar accused Waldrada of using magic to make Theutberga barren and attract Lothar to her.

The ongoing concern with superstition and pagan religious practice resulted in part from Christianity's continuing absorption of new non-Christian territories, and it is interesting to note that the Christian writers of the time were inconsistent in their willingness to give credence to the effectiveness of magic. For example, Archbishop Agobard of Lyon argued that weather magic was not real and that storms were the result either of natural causes or of divine intervention. Meanwhile, Archbishop Hincmar appeared to suggest that Waldrada had successfully employed magic to attract Lothar II and prevent Theutberga from having children. But as Christianity approached the end of its first millennium, even when Christian writers believed in the existence of genuine pagan magic, they were confident in the superiority of their own faith. For example, the *Decretum*, another important collection of church rulings by Burchard, Bishop of Worms (1000–25), forbade consultation with magicians and diviners, as well as the practice of pagan traditions, such as worshipping the sun and moon or reading special meaning into eclipses or other astronomical events. But even as Burchard acknowledged that superstitions and pagan magic might produce real effects, he derided those who employed them. His writings on the subject expressed the pre-eminence of Christian belief and faith, as well as a scoffing derision of the uneducated common people who engaged in these older practices. As Europe approached the high Middle Ages, superstition was still a popular feature of everyday life, but the church had achieved a degree of orthodoxy and influence that allowed its leaders to feel less threatened by paganism.

Superstition as demonic magic and witchcraft

The European period from 1000 to 1500 is one of enormous
upheaval and change, and a number of perilous events created the
kind of uncertainty and anxiety that are the foundation of belief
in magic and superstition. From the 11th to the 13th centuries, a
series of crusades were launched to recapture areas that had been
conquered by Muslim forces in the Middle East or were occupied
by pagan or heretical Christian groups in Europe. Typically, a
crusade was announced by the current pope, and several
European kings would contribute armies and send them to the
front. For example, Pope Urban II called for retaking the city of
Jerusalem from the Muslims, and in 1096, troops from northern
France, Lotharingia (present-day Netherlands, Belgium, and
Luxembourg), and Germany set out for the Middle East in the
first of many crusades over the next three centuries. The early
crusades were against Muslims but later ones took on heretical
Christian groups, such as the Albigensians of southern France
(1209–29) and the Hussites of Bohemia (1419–34).

The ancient world and the Middle Ages were often struck by
famines—prolonged periods of bad weather or bad crops that led
to insufficient supplies to get through the winter. Food shortages
affected all social classes, but peasants were particularly
vulnerable. Following two centuries of relative prosperity and
population growth, in the spring and summer of 1315, rains and
cold temperatures flooded fields, and killed many crops and farm
animals, and the worst famine in history descended upon
northern Europe and the British Isles. The Great Famine lingered
for three growing seasons until the weather finally returned to
normal in the summer of 1317, only to be followed by more cold
and harsh weather. Hunger was so great that people slaughtered
dairy animals, ate planting seed, and sent children away to fend
for themselves. A common theory suggests that *Hansel and Gretel*,
the famous fairy tale about two young children abandoned in the

forest by their parents, was based on this common practice during the Great Famine. A very bright comet was visible in the sky through much of 1317 and 1318, and naturally this celestial event was seen as a sign of bad crops ahead. It is difficult to know how many people died in the Great Famine, but it is estimated that in northern Europe, some cities saw a 10–25 per cent reduction in population. Furthermore, many of those who survived were weakened by scurvy, stunted growth, and other lasting problems, making them vulnerable to the next cataclysm to come along.

That cataclysm came later in the 14th century. The Black Plague, a much more deadly event, swept through a wide swathe of Asia and Europe. Although there is some controversy about the nature of the disease, it was probably bubonic plague caused by the *Yersinia pestis* bacterium. The first outbreak was in 1338–9 in a tiny village in China, near Lake Issyk Kul, along the Silk Road route from Asia to Europe, and it spread west and south carried by fleas who travelled in the fur of black rats. Some transmission appears to have been person to person, in which case contact could result in illness and death within forty-eight hours. The disease spread to India in 1344 and arrived in Constantinople and Egypt by 1347 and 1348 respectively. One hundred thousand people died in Cairo alone, and when it was carried by ship to England, close to half the population died. Within five years the population of Europe was reduced by a third.

The pandemic was made more frightening by the lack of agreement about what had caused it. The faculty of the medical school in Paris offered an astrological explanation, claiming the disease was produced by the conjunction of three planets in the constellation Aquarius, which produced a 'deadly corruption of the air'. In France and Germany, Jews were accused of poisoning the wells, which led to retaliation by angry mobs. Thousands of Jews who had not already succumbed to the plague were killed by fearful Christians.

During this period, there were also many changes in the organization and activities of the church. The power of the church became more institutionalized, in no small part by the ongoing series of crusades. Emperor Constantine had merged the church with imperial government, but when Urban II launched the first crusade, he elevated military combat to the high purpose of a contest between good and evil, and in so doing, further institutionalized the church's power.

In the mid-12th century, Gratian, a monk from Bologna, wrote the *Concordia Discordantium Canonum* ('Concord of Discordant Canons', now known as *Decretum Gratiani*), which, as its title suggests, attempted to reconcile all the previous sources of church law in a single text. This document soon became the leading authority on canon law, and several sections were devoted to the condemnation of harmful magic, sorcery, and astrology. Those who were found guilty of these forbidden practices were excommunicated or worse.

One feature of the increasing power of the church was the growing use of inquisitors to investigate reported cases of the use of magic or fortune telling. Often these were travelling judges who would appear in town, collect reports of suspicious goings-on, and conduct trials. In some cases, suspects were tortured to obtain confessions or submitted to judicial ordeals, like the one suffered by Theutberga's stand-in, to determine guilt or innocence. As odd as this approach might seem to modern observers, there was a certain similarity to jury trials today. The judicial ordeals were generally conducted in public, and a few days after the defendant had been burned by a hot poker or boiling water, the assembled crowd made a judgement as to whether the wound was healing normally. As a result, the defendant's popularity within the community affected the crowd's assessment of guilt or innocence. Furthermore, the stakes were quite high in these trials because those who made false accusations—accusations found lacking in evidence or popular support—were punished. As a result, accusers were more likely to escape retribution if they were of higher social standing than the accused.

Just as the church was gaining power, so were the purveyors of magic and superstition. Great advances in agriculture in the 9th and 10th centuries led to more plentiful food, increased trade, and expansion of European cities. Schools were established around the great cathedrals, and by the 11th and 12th centuries the first great universities emerged, including the University of Bologna (founded in 1088), University of Paris (later known as the Sorbonne, 1150), and University of Oxford (1167). By this time, many common forms of magic and superstition had become learned pursuits with extensive texts associated with them, and these topics were of great interest to early scholars. The rise of scholasticism fuelled a great interest in ancient magical texts, many of which had not been maintained by monks of the west but were preserved in the Byzantine Empire and by Arab and Jewish scholars. In the centuries following the life of the Prophet Muhammad (570–632 CE), the rise of Islam sparked the rapid spread of this new religious movement to the east and north of the Arabian peninsula and across the span of northern Africa. Islam's Golden Age, characterized by great economic, scientific, and cultural flourishing, began in the 8th century and continued to the 14th century, and although there were natural tensions among Christians, Muslims, and Jews, many European scholars produced Latin translations of Arab and Hebrew texts on astrology, astral magic, alchemy, and necromancy. In the case of astrology, some scholars made a distinction between the science of astronomy and the less well-regarded art of astrology, but as the University of Paris report on the Black Plague suggests, many considered both subjects legitimate. Scholars who studied these topics were sometimes accused of being magicians.

Beyond their academic study, sorcery and magic became much more professionalized activities. Perhaps because these topics had become more learned and drew upon foundational texts, some of the most common purveyors of sorcery and divination were lower-level clerics capitalizing on their association with the church establishment. Astrology, in particular, had become a much more established method of divination, and it was not uncommon for kings to employ astrologers. The royal astrologer's advice was not always heeded, but it was reported that the German king and emperor Frederick II (reigned 1215–50) would not conduct any major action without first consulting his astrologers. Interestingly, the same was said about Ronald Reagan, President of the United States over 700 years later, whose wife, Nancy Reagan, reportedly consulted a San Francisco astrologer before the president took any important action.

In the 12th century there was increased interest in the darker, demonic forms of magic. Often harmful spells cast against enemies would refer to a demon by name. Necromancy, the art of summoning the dead for the purpose of divination, was quite widely studied and employed. The practice typically involved spoken incantations, and because the secrets of necromancy were contained in various manuals, the professional necromancer had to be literate in Latin. As a result, its purveyors were almost always clerics who knew they were trafficking in forbidden practices. The idea that the dead—who, according to Christian doctrine, were permanent residents of either heaven or hell—could be summoned from one of these places to do the bidding of a necromancer was heretical, and those convicted of employing this dark art were punished and their necromancy texts destroyed.

Fears about demonic magic swelled during the 14th century, and accusations of demonic activity were common. Even those at the highest levels of society were not immune. In 1303 King Philip IV of France set off a power struggle with Pope Boniface VIII when he taxed the French church in an effort to fund the wars he was engaged in. Boniface eventually excommunicated the king, who responded by accusing the pope of heresy and of being under the control of a demon. Philip sent men to Italy to kidnap the pope from his residence. With the help of local townspeople Boniface managed to escape, but he was so shaken that he died soon after. In 1310 Philip tried to justify his actions by pushing the new pope, Clement V, to conduct a post-mortem trial of Boniface, this time charging him with consorting with not just one but three demons and another spirit. The trial never took place, but Philip was not finished. In another effort to seize funds and property, he levelled his next attack against the Knights Templar.

The Knights of the Temple of Solomon, or Knights Templar, were a group of French knight-monks who emerged as a crusading order during the early crusades, and over a series of many campaigns acquired considerable land and wealth. However, the last crusade was in 1291, and by 1307, Philip hatched a plan to take the Templars' property. He charged the Templars with a number of crimes, including heresy, sodomy, and worshipping demons—in particular, a demonic head known as Bophomet. Most, if not all, of these charges were false, but under torture a number of leaders of the Templars admitted to crimes which they later recanted. In 1312, Pope Clement made an arrangement with Philip to disband the Templars—avoiding a formal trial—but in 1314 a number of Templars, including the grand master of the order Jacques de Molay, were burned at the stake for recanting their prior confessions (see Figure 4).

Although they may not actually have been demon worshippers, the Knights Templar have played another more famous role in the history of superstition. Because de Molay and a large number of knights were arrested on Friday, 13 October 1307, the Knights Templar are cited as one of the many theories about the origin of the unlucky Friday the 13th superstition. The source of the modern Friday the 13th superstition has been hotly debated, and as we will see, the Knights Templar theory is probably not the strongest explanation.

4. Philip IV ordering the burning of the Knights Templar.

In the episode of the Knights Templar we can see the beginnings
of a new phase of concern about magic and superstition.
Destructive, malevolent magic had always been treated harshly,
but it was primarily described as an individual enterprise. A local
sorcerer or magician was charged with practising unsavoury arts
and was excommunicated or killed. But in the 14th and 15th
centuries a much more ominous threat emerged that would be a
considerable worry for the next four centuries: conspiratorial
groups of demon-worshipping black magicians. In particular, the
15th century saw a rising fear of alleged secret societies of witches.
It was one thing to be a member of a heretical religious group,

which had been the motivation for a number of holy wars, but it was quite another to believe that there were members of your own community who met secretly to perform blasphemous rituals and summon demonic forces.

Popular belief in witches had been a part of European culture going back to Circe of Homer's *Odyssey* and beyond, but from 900 to 1400 the church did not acknowledge the existence of witches, much less engage in witch trials. During this period of increased concern about demonic magic, the official stance began to change. A number of texts about witchcraft were published in the 15th century that helped to spread knowledge of this dreaded phenomenon. By far the most important of these was the *Malleus Maleficarum* (The Hammer of Witches) published in 1486 by Heinrich Kramer, a Dominican monk, and Jacob Sprenger, a scholar, both of whom were German inquisitors. The subtitle of *Malleus* translates as 'which destroys witches and their heresy as with a two-edged sword', and the book included methods for investigating and trying suspected witches.

Kramer and Sprenger proposed a theory of witches that came to be regarded as accepted Christian doctrine on the subject. They asserted that witchcraft was heretical and that witches must be killed. Furthermore, merely doubting the existence of witches was also heretical. The *Malleus* provided an explanation for the spread of witches that involved an elaborate system of demonology. Demons were presumed to be angels who had fallen from heaven and possessed varying powers beyond that of humans. Demons were incapable of procreation, but succubi and incubi would often have sex with humans. A demon of the female succubus form could collect sperm from a man by having intercourse with him, at which point she had a choice. She could transform into a male incubus and have sex with a female human, but that approach required the incubus to go on to serve the witch who resulted from this union. If the demon preferred not to be teamed up with a witch, she would transfer the collected semen to an incubus who had been assigned to the witch. The incubus in turn would have sex with the woman—being careful to choose a time when the stars were propitious for the production of male or female witches—after which the demon would be commanded by the witch.

Many other witchcraft manuals were published both before and after *Malleus*, some of which addressed widely debated questions about how witches fly and the nature of the witches' sabbath—neither of which were covered by Kramer and Sprenger—but one of the *Malleus'* most important influences was to promote a gendered notion of witchcraft. Kramer and Sprenger claimed that witches were more often women because their deficient intellect made them more vulnerable, and—in contrast to the relative moderation of men—women were prone to the extremes of good and evil. Despite the obvious contradiction that many of the most common magicians and sorcerers were male clerics, the stereotype of the female witch would come to dominate in subsequent centuries.

Malleus was an enormous success and remained popular over the next two centuries—at times, second in sales only to the Bible. It became a script for a long dark period of fear and suspicion because, in addition to helping to create the mythology of demons, witches, and witchcraft, it outlined the procedures for identifying suspects and conducting trials and executions. Furthermore, it carried the authority of the church behind it. However, when the witch trials finally ended, so did an almost 2,000-year period of applying the label of superstition to unacceptable or foreign religious practices. But we are getting ahead of ourselves. Superstition and magic went through a number of additional transformations before arriving at the Age of Reason.

Chapter 3
The secularization of superstition

The five centuries beginning with the 14th and ending with the 18th took European history from the Middle Ages, through the Enlightenment, and into the first two centuries of the scientific age, which would mark the final turn in the meaning of superstition. This passage involved the flourishing of the humanities that we associate with the Renaissance, the Protestant Reformation, and great advances in science—as well as deadly wars, plagues, inquisitions, and witch hunts. But the culmination of this period would produce the Enlightenment, a new age of reason, and a different form of attack on superstition and magic.

The age of mages

The Renaissance had its beginnings in the late 13th century in Florence, Italy, with a great wave of humanism and renewed interest in classical philosophy, art, and science. The growth of cities with larger professional and merchant classes, combined with the wider availability of books, thanks to new printing methods, promoted an interest in a number of humanist topics. Many lawyers and notaries had come into contact with classical texts as part of their training, and they began to amass personal libraries and study and teach the humanist fields of grammar, rhetoric, history, poetry, and moral philosophy. The tools of education were freed from the bonds of the church, and by this time, many classical Greek and Roman texts had been translated into vernacular Italian, making them more widely accessible. Furthermore, many Italian libraries were open to any scholars who wished to use them, and an active trade in books greatly democratized the study of a variety of topics. The art of the time reflected a new emphasis on realism, most notably seen in the work of Leonardo da Vinci (1452–1519), who was himself the kind of polymath we associate with Renaissance humanism.

Despite all these advances, magic and superstition persisted. The average European employed a number of magical methods in everyday life and frequently would consult with cunning individuals who were thought to be talented in spells and divination. Meanwhile, the church continued its attacks on any form of magic that might involve the work of demons. But the new humanism of the Renaissance brought a number of long neglected texts to light, and the study of magic became a popular topic. The period produced several famous magicians or mages who wrote extensively on the subject. On the one hand, the humanist study of magic was a kind of elite discipline, distinct from the popular superstition and magic of the streets. On the other hand, the mages avoided drawing fire from the church and its inquisitors by concentrating on accepted forms of magic that employed 'natural' forces rather than the power of demons.

The Byzantine Empire, the last vestige of the Roman Empire, fell in 1453 when the Ottomans conquered Constantinople. One of the effects of the defeat was the dispersion of a number of ancient texts that had been held in the capital city. In particular, a Byzantine monk brought a group of texts of esoteric philosophy known as the *Corpus Hermeticum* to the Medici family in Florence. These texts were written in Greek and were attributed to Hermes Trismegistus (Thrice-great Hermes), and although they were Greek mystical texts from the 2nd or 3rd century, their original source was thought to be the much older wisdom of the Egyptian god Toth, whom the Greeks associated with the god

Hermes. These Hermetic works were eventually translated into Latin by Marsilio Ficino (1433–99), a Florentine scholar supported by the patronage of the Medici family. Ficino was an important figure in the 15th century during a period of renewed interest in Plato, and he had already published a Latin translation of Plato's works by the time the *Corpus Hermeticum* came into his hands. After translating the *Corpus*, he went on to publish his own three-volume book *De Vita Libri Tres* (Three Books of Life), the last volume of which was *De Vita Coelitus Comparanda* (On Life Connected to the Heavens), which dealt with the nature of astral forces.

Ficino's text was primarily a description of a medical system that rested upon control of the body and all terrestrial objects by celestial ones. His system involved three levels of influence. On the highest plane was the angelic or intellectual world of the spirits. Below this were the stars and planets, and finally Earthly things. Between and among these levels were the *spiritus mundi* (world spirits) which linked them together and allowed the influence of one level upon another. According to Ficino, the magician's task was to influence the *spiritus* in ways that would affect the planets and, in turn, events on Earth. For example, the planet Venus might be implored to instigate a romance. When it came to the treatment of physical ailments, the planets could be influenced by various foods or the burning of incense. Some minerals were also thought to have natural connections with the planets, such as gold with the sun. Ficino's magic was presented as completely natural and part of a Neoplatonic attempt to understand the construction of the universe and, thus, not in conflict with religious dogma.

Several other 15th-century Neoplatonic humanists became experts on magic—each with his own unique approach. One of these was Giovanni Pico della Mirandola (1463–94), a brilliant and audacious scholar who lived a short but remarkable life. Born into a wealthy family, he showed early academic promise and was

educated in Bologna and Padua, eventually becoming a colleague
of Ficino's in Florence and, like him, gaining the financial support
of Lorenzo de' Medici. Pico's approach was Platonic in the sense
that he hoped to reconcile ancient sources of wisdom with
Christianity, but in addition to an interest in Hermetic traditions,
Pico was fascinated with the Kabbalah, a mystical tradition within
Judaism. Pico hoped to merge the Kabbalah with Christian
doctrine, as well as to convert Jews to Christianity.

Pico appears to have been a remarkably bold scholar because he
wrote a collection of propositions called *900 Theses*, which he
intended to defend against all comers. The idea was to move to
Rome, publish *900 Theses*, and offer to pay the transportation
costs of anyone who wished to come to Rome and challenge him
in debate, but the plan hit an early snag. On the way to Rome,
Pico initiated a love affair with the wife of one of Lorenzo de'
Medici's cousins and was only able to escape safely with the
assistance of Lorenzo himself. Eventually, Pico arrived in Rome,
but before his debate competition could get under way, Pope
Innocent VIII put an end to it. The pope declared thirteen of
Pico's theses heretical, particularly those dealing with magic and
the Kabbalah. In response, Pico agreed to remove those thirteen
theses—refusing any suggestion they were, in fact, wrong—but to
no avail. The pope eventually declared the entire *900 Theses*
heretical. Pico had hoped to reconcile all the diverse systems of
ancient and medieval wisdom, but the church establishment
would have none of it. As a result, Pico's *900 Theses* became the
first book to be universally banned by the church, and almost all
copies were burned.

But Pico's troubles were not over. The pope assembled an
inquisition, and Pico was forced to denounce the *Theses* and was
censured. He fled to France, where, at the request of French papal
emissaries, he was arrested and imprisoned. Again, Lorenzo de'
Medici intervened, and Pico was allowed to live quietly in
Florence under Lorenzo's protection. However, in 1494, two years

after Lorenzo's death, Pico died at the age of 31 under suspicious circumstances on the same day that Charles VIII of France marched into Florence. In 2007, Pico's body was exhumed and analysed by scientists, who concluded that he had succumbed to arsenic poisoning, probably at the behest of Piero de' Medici, Lorenzo's son and successor.

There is one more aspect of Pico's work that we should note before leaving him. During his final years in Florence, a regressive ideology that was critical of the new Renaissance became popular in the city, and Pico fell under its sway. He renounced his previous preoccupations with magic, ancient Hermetic wisdom, and the Kabbalah as the fascinations of his youth and devoted his time to the defence of Christian orthodoxy. During this period Pico wrote his last great work, *Disputationes Adversus Astrologiam Divinatricem* (Treatise Against Predictive Astrology). Despite the fact that his colleague Ficino was an astrologer, Pico attacked astrological divination on the grounds that it was too deterministic. Christian dogma required that people have free will, and, according to Pico, astrology was based on the idea that astral forces determined events on Earth.

Not all of the Renaissance *magi* were from Florence. Another important figure was the German lawyer, physician, and philosopher Heinrich Cornelius Agrippa von Nettesheim (1486–1535), who began studying magic while still a young man. Agrippa eventually published one of the most influential magical texts of the time, *De Occulta Philosophia* (On Occult Philosophy), which took a Neoplatonic approach similar to that of Ficino and Pico in an effort to reconcile the magical wisdom of the ancients with Christian doctrine.

Agrippa's text was very popular and served to spread knowledge of the magical arts, particularly in northern Europe, but Agrippa's career put him in conflict with inquisitors. When he tried to get the *De Occulta* published by a printer in Cologne, a Dominican inquisitor proclaimed the book heretical. Agrippa vigorously defended himself before the city council, and ultimately the archbishop overruled the inquisitor, clearing the path for publication in 1533. But late in life and particularly after his death, Agrippa was accused of being a black magician in league with the devil. Other Renaissance *magi* of the time were careful to associate themselves with white, non-demonic magic, but Agrippa's *De Occulta* described a universe that was inhabited by both good demons (angels) and bad demons, making him susceptible to the criticism that he engaged in black magic and witchcraft.

Later Agrippa's life and work would be rolled into the German myth of Faustus, which was based on a historical figure, Johann Georg Faust (*c.*1480–1540), who, according to legend, made a bargain with the devil in order to acquire magical powers. In Christopher Marlowe's 1592 play *Doctor Faustus*, Faust boasts that he

> Will be as cunning as Agrippa was,
> Whose shadow made all Europe honour him.

Common superstitions of the Renaissance era

All of this academic study of magic was happening in the rather rarefied environments of the nobility and the scholarly elite, but, just as they had since the beginning of human history, the common people continued to engage in many activities that were much closer to what today we would call superstition. As Christianity spread throughout Europe and beyond, the church of the Middle Ages was forced to look the other way when many of their new converts clung to their old pagan rituals and magical incantations. As we have seen, the world remained a harsh and unforgiving place, and the uncertainties of the weather, crops, illness, and injury kept various luck-enhancing rituals and systems of divination alive. As the church became more institutionalized and dominant in the Middle Ages and Renaissance, many common superstitions adhered to Christian rituals, putting the church hierarchy in an awkward position. Many Christian writers dismissed these practices as superstitious, but because they drew attention to the church and were in many cases expressions of genuine faith, the establishment often allowed or even encouraged a number of popular religiously based superstitions.

Although Christianity distinguished itself from pagan religions by a rejection of polytheism, it provided a serviceable substitute: saints. Indeed, in many cases the tombs of local saints became shrines that attracted a kind of cultic worship that was similar to the older Roman temples. The church establishment was quick to point out that saints had only the powers granted to them by God, but the possibility of saintly magic was central to the idea of sainthood and the process of canonization. Even today, to be canonized as a saint, the Vatican must certify that the candidate for sainthood caused at least one posthumous miracle. For example, in 1987 Edith Stein, a German Jew who had converted to Catholicism in 1922 but was killed in the death camps at Auschwitz in 1942, was beatified as a martyr. At the time of her death, she was a Carmelite nun and had taken the name 'Sr Teresa Benedicta of the Cross'. In 1987, a young girl was said to have been cured of liver disease when her family prayed to Sr Teresa Benedicta of the Cross, and after medical testimony was offered in support of the case, Pope John Paul II canonized Stein as a saint.

Given the aura of miracles that surrounded saints, it is not surprising that believers sought them out for medical cures and other benefits. In the Middle Ages, there was a lively trade in saints' relics, which were purported to have miraculous powers derived from their association with a saint. Skulls, bones, and pieces of clothing attributed to saints were—and in many cases still are—said to possess special powers.

One of the longest-running practices of saint worship is associated with St Christopher, who, according to legend, carried the young Jesus across a river. Many churches in the Middle Ages had depictions of St Christopher on their walls, and those who gazed upon his image were said to be protected against illness and death that day. Because St Christopher is the patron saint of travellers, there continues to be a market for St Christopher medals to be worn around the neck or clipped to automobile sun visors. Similarly, for reasons that are not entirely clear, legend has it that St Joseph, who was Mary's husband and Jesus's foster father, is a talented real estate agent. It is believed that burying a St Joseph statuette—often upside down in the front lawn—will hasten the sale of the family home. On the internet one can find a variety of St Joseph home-selling kits.

In the Middle Ages and the Renaissance, many of the objects associated with the church were thought to have magical powers. Holy water was one of the most popular of all magical religious objects—undoubtedly because it was common and could be used in so many ways. In addition, there were established church procedures for blessing homes, cattle, crops, and people headed out on journeys, and often these would involve a priest or other church official applying holy water. Holy water was most often encountered in the baptismal font, and because baptism was a cleansing ritual and a form of exorcism, holy water was thought to possess the power to drive away demons. Church officials typically rejected the idea that drinking holy water could cure disease and privately believed it was not as useful as was commonly thought, but they generally did nothing to discourage these beliefs as long as they were based in Christian faith. During a violent storm in Canterbury, England, in 1543, town residents reportedly ran to the church to obtain holy water to spread on their houses in the hope that it would protect against lightning or other damage.

The communion host was also thought to have substantial power. Congregants who did not swallow the bread and carried it out of the church were thought to possess an object capable of strong magic. The host was used to put out fires, cure swine fever, and cast love spells. Many other consecrated objects reportedly had a variety of magical properties, including consecrated salt, candles, and palms used on Palm Sunday. Wax from the candles that were blessed on the day of the Purification of the Blessed Virgin (also known as Candlemas) was sometimes inscribed during mass on St Agatha's day. Because of St Agatha's association with putting out fires, any house containing pieces of this wax was thought to be protected from fire. Few of these applications were sanctioned by the church, but they were widely endorsed by the people. Because the church was a natural treasury of blessed objects, theft became a common problem. In some cases, church fonts were locked up and other precautions were taken to avoid loss of religious items.

All of this was, in some sense, an understandable outgrowth of the church, which tended to emphasize its supernatural qualities. The mass placed great emphasis on the priest, and the assembled believers were relatively passive observers. The rituals, prayers, and, above all, the priestly act of transubstantiation—the magical transformation of simple bread and wine into the actual body and blood of Jesus—promoted the idea that there was magic in the church and that mere presence at mass might bring luck and prosperity to the attendants. The mysteriousness of the rituals was probably enhanced by the fact that most of the parishioners did not understand the Latin phrases they were hearing. For centuries, magicians and wizards had uttered incantations in Egyptian, Hebrew, and other foreign languages.

But in the everyday world of village life, there were many common superstitious practices that came neither from the scholarly magicians nor from the magic of the church. As they had for centuries, local magicians, wizards, and cunning people offered services that had been passed along via spell books or word of mouth. Again, there was an aspect of social hierarchy that divided the academics and the church from these more mundane practitioners, who continued to be quite active during the Renaissance. In addition, some practices were well known and could be employed without the help of a professional.

The search for buried treasure was a much more common enterprise than it is today. Because there were no banks, people often hid their riches in boxes under their beds or buried them underground. According to popular belief, many people made happy reversals of fortune when they discovered hidden treasure under the ruins of a burnt-out house or buried on the side of a hill. The search for wealth did not require the use of magic, but searchers often consulted a magician or conjuror for guidance.

Just as in the case of ancient binding spells, magic in the Middle Ages and Renaissance was often aimed at kindling or extinguishing the bond of love. Using old spell books as guides, practitioners offered potions or incantations that could turn anyone's affections in the direction of the client. For a fee, village magicians offered to secure new spouses for widows and widowers.

Finally, fortune telling in all of its various forms remained a popular vocation. The vagaries of weather and the success or failure of crops were always of vital concern, but fortune tellers were also frequently consulted when the client was troubled by some difficult matter or pending decision—as they still are today. In these cases, the village wizard undoubtedly engaged in a process not unlike the cold reading methods that have always been used by psychics and palm readers. The client often arrived with a plan in mind, and the magician's job was to detect the client's initial inclination and gently guide them to it. As much as any actual divination that might be involved, the magician's service was to shift some of the burden of responsibility for a difficult dilemma off the client and onto the mage.

Superstition as Catholic ritual

After over a millennium of domination, establishment Christianity experienced a radical rebellion, and the pejorative label 'superstition' was turned in a new direction. In this case, the rebels raised the shibboleth of superstition against the Roman Church itself. Ironically, this conflict represented an important step toward the eventual secularization of superstition.

As we have seen, over the course of its long history, the Roman Church developed many rituals that were only distinguishable from traditional incantations and charms by their Christian content and ecclesiastical sanction. Furthermore, these rituals tended to place the power of magic in the hands of priests and other clerics. The church had not rejected magic so much as incorporated enough of it into its repertoire of sacraments and traditions to satisfy the parishioners. Non-Christian magic was either ignored or condemned as dangerous superstition.

Then came the Protestants who called out the wizardry of the church of Rome as superstition. When Martin Luther, a professor of moral theology at the University of Wittenberg and a town preacher, sent his *Ninety-Five Theses* to Albert of Brandenburg, the Archbishop of Mainz, on 31 October 1517, launching the Protestant Reformation, his first attack was levelled at the church's use of indulgences, which, when granted, reduced the amount of time spent in Purgatory. By the late Middle Ages, the granting of indulgences was widely abused and commercialized. Corrupt church officials and professional 'pardoners' took money in exchange for the granting of indulgences, and this practice was harshly attacked by Luther and other like-minded reformers. An example of this kind of morally questionable behaviour can be seen in Chaucer's character of the Pardoner in *The Canterbury Tales*.

Martin Luther started the movement with his critique of indulgences, but he and other Protestant writers soon took up a variety of issues, including what they considered the superstitious practices of the church of Rome. One area of attack was the consecrated objects used by the Catholics. Protestant critics argued that only God could bless an object. All things created by

45

God were good when created and could only become good or bad as a result of their use. The superstitious practice of consecrating items was idolatrous and the work of the devil.

Some writers made a direct connection between those who consecrated water, salt, bread, and the conjurors and sorcerers who trafficked in common magic. Protestants argued that the act of consecrating sacramental objects provided the devil with additional means to deceive the believers. The devil brought on misfortune, only to appear to take it away when people engaged in idolatrous acts, such as worshiping consecrated objects. Thus, according to these Protestant critics, the magic of the church and simple spells and incantations shared a common demonology.

Protestants retained some of the rituals of the Catholic Church, in particular baptism and the Eucharist, but they described these acts as simple expressions of the parishioner's faith. The idea that a cleric's incantations could change the nature of an object was rejected, and worship was greatly demystified.

But even as they strove to purge the new movement of superstition, Protestants faced some of the same pressures encountered by the church of the early Middle Ages and, for that matter, the elites of Greece and Rome before them. The demand for magical incantations to ward off bad crops, disease, and fires was just too great to permit a complete cold turkey rejection. As a result, some of the rituals associated with these needs were disconnected from consecrated objects. For example, an annual ritual of blessing the fields would be converted into an opportunity to pray and worship outdoors, or alternatively, a special sermon would be given on these important days. Although parishioners believed these practices had a similar influence on events, the clergy could content themselves that there was no idolatry or demonic influence involved.

The age of heretics, wars, and witches

The Reformation coincided with—and in some ways led directly to—a long and devastating period in European history. As we have seen, throughout the later Middle Ages, inquisitors were busy conducting trials and punishing heretics and those suspected of demonic magic. Torture had been sanctioned by Pope Innocent IV in 1251, and Dominican monks became quite skilled at its use. From the late Middle Ages well into the 16th and 17th centuries, a variety of gruesome methods of torture and execution were popular throughout Europe. Heretics and criminal suspects were stretched on racks, burned, impaled on pikes, and sawn in half. The Spanish Inquisition began in the late 15th century and continued for three and a half centuries. It was particularly active during the period from 1480 to 1530, during which the primary goal was ferreting out Jews and Muslims who were thought to have faked their conversion to Christianity. In 1492, King Ferdinand and Queen Isabella expelled thousands of Jews from Spain, and those converts to Christianity who remained were under threat of the inquisitor, who often tortured his victims to obtain a confession (see Figure 5). Christianity functioned as a state religion, and all those who entered from lands where other religions predominated were required to convert. Jews, who had already suffered many centuries of discrimination and—in the case of the Crusades—genocidal extermination, were often thought to be secretly continuing to practise their forbidden religion. Inquisitors also targeted Christian heretics, including a variety of Protestant groups, and those who violated moral laws, such as bigamy and sodomy. The Spanish Inquisition had an estimated death toll of 350,000.

Starting soon after publication of the *Ninety-Five Theses* and extending well into the 17th century, Europe was swept by a period of violent conflict now known as the Wars of Religion. Many of these wars were direct conflicts between Protestants and

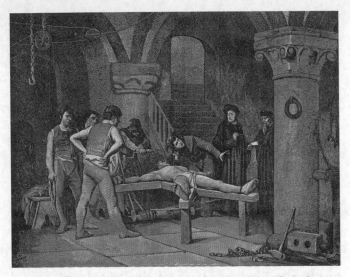

5. A man dressed in a loincloth is tortured on the rack with a priest bending over him to extract a confession. Wood engraving by B. Pug after J.M.

Catholics and, and as a result, are sometimes called the Wars of Reformation and Counter-Reformation. These included the German Peasants' War (1524–26), the Tudor Conquest of Ireland (1529–1603), the French Wars of Religion (1562–98), the Eighty Years War (1568–1648), the English Civil War (1642–8), and the Thirty Years War (1618–48), among many others. Although most of the wars of this period started over or were primarily about religion, others were conflicts about royal succession or wars of independence. The longer wars, in particular, were fought over a mixture of complaints.

This period was one of the bloodiest in European history. The French Wars of Religion, which pitted Protestant Huguenot followers of John Calvin in the south and west of France against Catholics in the north, left an estimated three million people dead from violence, famine, or disease. The most deadly of the

Religious Wars was the Thirty Years War in Germany between the Catholic Habsburg states of the revived Holy Roman Empire and the Protestant anti-Habsburg countries. The war eventually involved much of Europe, from England and Scotland to Denmark and Norway, and left an estimated 5.75 million people dead, a total which, as a proportion of the world's population, is double the death rate of the First World War.

As you will recall, the inquisitors Heinrich Kramer and Jacob Sprenger published the *Malleus Maleficarum* in 1486, but two years earlier Kramer and Sprenger had complained to Pope Innocent VIII (1484–92) that their efforts to conduct witch trials had often been resisted by local authorities. As a result, the pope issued the bull *Summis Desiderantes Affectibus* (Desiring with Greatest Ardour), in which he expressed great concern about the reports of witchcraft in Germany and authorized Kramer and Sprenger to pursue their inquisitions. Thus, the church was officially on record authorizing the hunting and killing of witches. Although in Spain and Portugal inquisitions remained focused on rooting out heresy and were rarely directed at presumed witches, elsewhere in northern Europe, England, Scotland, and in the British colonies, the years of the Religious Wars coincided with a widespread fear of witchcraft and a surge in trials and executions. The *Malleus* and other witch manuals were very popular, but there were a few sceptics who questioned at least some aspects of the mythology of witches. For example, the legal scholar Ulrich Molitor published *De Lamiis et Phitonicis Mulieribus* (Of Witches and Women Who Prophesy), in which he rejected the reality of witches' sabbaths and witch flight, but he otherwise supported the view that some women consorted with the devil. Furthermore, his differing positions on these issues did not deter him from supporting the execution of witches and heretics.

Over the years, estimates of the number of people killed during the years of the witch craze have varied widely, but current estimates put the number between 60,000 and 100,000 deaths, with 75 to 85 per cent of victims being women. Approximately half of all people tried as witches were executed. Scholars have offered a number of possible explanations for the witch phenomena of the 16th and 17th centuries. For example, the ongoing conflict between Protestants and Catholics seems like an obvious possibility; however, witchcraft was not a point of ideological conflict. Both sides engaged in witch hunts and executions. However, in those areas where Catholicism was thriving, the church was unable to gain much public support for inquisitions. Witch hunts were much more active in areas, such as England, France, and Germany, where Protestantism challenged Catholic domination. In contrast, witch hunts were relatively rare in places such as Ireland, Spain, and Italy, where Catholicism was more securely in command. It is likely that witch hunts were used first by Catholics but eventually by both sides as a way of showing the populace that the church was protecting them from the imagined evil of witches. What the church previously considered a superstitious belief was now given great credibility and indeed *not* believing in witches was considered heresy.

Superstition as bad science

In the 16th and much of the 17th centuries, Europe was a dark and deadly place. The conflict, fear, and suspicion of the age were, in one sense, the perfect atmosphere for the maintenance of superstitious beliefs, but they also led to a much more modern view of magic, demons, and the supernatural.

Eventually Europeans grew tired of killing each other for not having the right religious beliefs. The Peace of Westphalia, signed in 1648, ended the Thirty Years War and established some general principles of autonomy among nations and a framework for religious coexistence. Each prince could determine the religion of his territories—Catholicism, Lutheranism, or Calvinism—but Christians whose sect did not match the local state religion would be allowed to practise in relative peace and freedom. Some of this religious tolerance came as a direct reaction against the illogic of the Religious Wars. In 1553, John Calvin had the Spanish physician and theologian Michael Servetus burned at the stake in Geneva for the crime of heresy: Servetus opposed infant baptism and questioned the concept of the trinity. The French preacher and theologian Sebastian Castellio accused Calvin of murder and wrote a passionate but reasoned argument against the killing of Servetus.

> If Servetus had attacked you by arms, you had rightly been
> defended by the magistrate; but since he opposed you in writings,
> why did you oppose them with iron and flame? Do you call this the
> defence of the pious magistrate?...To kill a man is not to defend a
> doctrine, but to kill a man. When the Genevans killed Servetus they
> did not defend a doctrine; they killed a man. The defence of
> doctrine is not the affair of the magistrate but of the doctor. What
> has the sword to do with doctrine? (Sebastian Castellio, *Contra
> Libellum Calvini* (Against Calvin's Book), 1562)

In Castellio's conflict with Calvin we can see the beginnings of the religious tolerance that would become law in the Westphalia Peace a century later and an essential part of the Enlightenment to come. Castellio believed that heretics were wrong and bad for the church, but he did not believe they should be executed for their beliefs. The correct response to a heretic was reasoning and persuasion.

The tolerance built into the Peace of Westphalia was one of a number of 17th- and 18th-century changes that created a different atmosphere in Europe. For the first time, there was a growing sense that philosophy could be separated from religion, and the French philosophers Voltaire (1694–1778) and Jean-Jacques Rousseau (1712–78) argued that morality should be based on reason rather than religion. There was increased support for the idea that constitutional governments were superior to those based on religious authority and for the values of religious tolerance and individual freedom.

This was also a time of great advancement in science, or natural philosophy, as it was known, although the course of progress did not always run true. In 1543, Nicolaus Copernicus first published his theory that the Sun and not the Earth was the centre of the 'universe', in opposition to the established Aristotelian view. The Danish astronomer Tycho Brahe supported traditional geocentrism, but Johannes Kepler, like Copernicus, was a heliocentrist who worked out a number of details of the Copernican view. In 1633, the great Italian astronomer Galileo Galilei was brought before the Roman Inquisition to face both scientific and religious charges for his support of the heliocentric view, and in what was seen as a late effort on the part of the Christian establishment to push back against the advance of objective natural philosophy, Galileo, who was 69 years old and ill, was forced to recant his prior views under threat of torture and spend the rest of his life under house arrest.

But the ideas that led to the modern world continued to spread. British scientist Francis Bacon (1561–1626), French philosopher and mathematician René Descartes (1596–1650), and British mathematician and physicist Isaac Newton (1643–1727) supported the growing view that nature could be understood through observation and logic and without reference to divine intervention. The chemist Robert Boyle (1627–91) challenged many of the basic assumptions of alchemy but is primarily known for his discovery of Boyle's Law, which describes the relationship between the pressure and volume of a gas. He was also a founder of the Royal Society, which conducted a number of experimental investigations. As is still true today, the emerging scientists sometimes clung to non-scientific ideas. Newton is often credited with having launched the new era of science, but he wrote many works on alchemy and supported a view of gravitational attraction based on occult forces. Nonetheless, the world-view that grew out of the work of Bacon, Descartes, Boyle, and Newton was largely based in materialism and the belief that truth was available to all and need not come down from church authorities.

Thus, the word superstition made its last turn of meaning. The epithet of superstition had already been hurled at religious targets when the Protestants accused Catholics of engaging in heretical superstitious incantations and rituals, and the new natural philosophers of the Enlightenment continued to target the magical aspects of Christianity. But for the first time, the label began to take on its modern meaning of 'bad science'. Both the supernatural powers of consecrated objects and the spells of the local magician were superstitious, not because they were dangerous or unauthorized forms of religion but because they did not make sense according to the new logic of science. In the Enlightenment view, centuries of church rule had stunted the process of human flourishing. Using the word in its anti-religion sense, the French philosopher Denis Diderot (1713–84) wrote, 'When superstition is allowed to perform the task of old age in dulling the human temperament, we can say goodbye to excellence in poetry, painting, and music.'

The Enlightenment was a new age of reason and scientific experimentation, and one of the fruits of the period was a sense of general optimism and reduced uncertainty. The much broader use of insurance in the business world removed a degree of risk from running a business or sending a ship out to sea. Advances in agriculture reduced the incidence of famine, and improved understanding of anatomy and medicine promoted greater confidence in doctors. By modern standards not all of this confidence was justified. Well into the 19th century, bloodletting remained a very common treatment for any number of diseases. But the general sense of improved autonomy and control—even if it was an illusion—created a psychological environment that reduced the reliance on magic and superstition.

Despite the increasing secularization of the 17th and
18th centuries, the practice of witch hunts, trials, and executions
would not die out completely until the late 18th century, and even
then, it wasn't because people no longer believed in witches.
The declining obsession with witches was largely due to changes
in the administration of justice. Witchcraft was still considered
real, but greater central control over the judicial process led to
fewer convictions. Witch panics were a local affair, and it became
clear that, in an emotional zeal to kill witches, many people were
being convicted of things they did not do. For example, a panic in
the German city of Würzburg led to the death of hundreds of
people between 1627 and 1629, including several members of the
nobility, forty-three members of the clergy, and forty-one children.
It was common to torture suspected witches until they produced
the names of other witches and accomplices, a technique that
greatly expanded the number of suspects. Torture was eventually
restricted or prohibited—not on humanitarian grounds but due to
a growing understanding that it produced unreliable results.
Similarly, central authorities often reviewed local proceedings and
demanded more substantial evidence of guilt. These legal reforms
had the effect of decreasing convictions and executions.

Anna Göldi of the Swiss canton of Glarus is thought to be the last
witch killed in Europe by a sanctioned trial. She admitted to the
crime of witchcraft after being hung by her thumbs with stones
tied to her feet and was subsequently beheaded with a sword on
13 June 1782. In 2008, the Glarus parliament acknowledged her
execution was a miscarriage of justice and officially exonerated
her. Today there is a lasting memorial in her honour at the Glarus
courthouse—two lit lamps representing violations of human rights
throughout the world.

Borrowing a phrase from the poet Friedrich Schiller, the
20th-century German sociologist Max Weber proposed that
science and the Enlightenment had led to 'the disenchantment of
the world', by which he meant a diminished influence of both

religion and magic. In Weber's view reason and scientific inquiry had produced a more secular, more bureaucratic world, untethered to traditional religious values. Time has revealed that Weber's assessment is both right and wrong. It is wrong because the Enlightenment and the rise of science has not eliminated superstition. Far from it. As we will see, our world is more secular and less mysterious than it was before the Enlightenment, but both religion and superstition are alive and well. Weber's assessment is correct in the sense that, after the Enlightenment, explanations of natural events that depend on God's influence, demons, or magic forces were no longer acceptable. For the first time, science and reason provided the standard against which a belief or action was judged to be superstitious or non-superstitious.

Ancient religious ideas of demonic magic have not completely died out. I recall some years ago when a Christian journalist called me for comment on the fact that the Washington, DC basketball team had chosen the name The Wizards. She seemed very troubled about this fact. Later some evangelical Christians sounded an alarm about children reading Harry Potter books because of their positive depictions of witchcraft—even going so far as to sponsor book burnings. But, with these few exceptions, the new standard for superstition and magical belief is science, and—for now, at least—it seems unlikely that the concept of superstition will return to its prior meaning of 'bad religion'.

Chapter 4
Superstition in the modern world

The secularization of superstition began to take hold in the Enlightenment and the years of rapid scientific progress that followed. With rare exceptions, the label 'superstitious' was now applied to unscientific beliefs that defied reason. But science took some time to develop into the sophisticated collection of methods we know today, and, despite the growing dominance of scientific reasoning, superstition, pseudoscience, and magical thinking did not go away. Indeed, for reasons we will encounter in Chapter 5, they may never go away. In this chapter we turn to the kinds of superstitions that survive today, but first we will encounter a social movement that kept supernatural beliefs alive before science became a more mature enterprise at the beginning of the 20th century.

19th-century spiritualism

Although witch hunts ended in the 18th century and intellectual elites largely discarded the world of magic, spells, and demons, new forms of popular supernatural belief emerged in the 19th century to fill the gap. In Europe and especially in the United States a new wave of spiritualism began in the mid-19th century, and although this phenomenon had much earlier roots, it was also a unique reflection of a number of contemporary social movements.

On 31 March 1848 Kate and Margaret (Maggie) Fox, two teenage sisters living with their parents in Hydesville, New York, began to hear rapping sounds that they attributed to a spirit of a murdered pedlar named 'Mr Splitfoot'. Mr Splitfoot would rap in response to specific questions and appeared to have remarkable knowledge of the Fox family and other matters. Soon it became clear that this phenomenon was not limited to the family's Hydesville home. Kate and Maggie, as well as their older sister Leah, could communicate with other spirits in any location, and they submitted to a number of tests in Rochester, NY, some of which were held in a large hall before an audience of 400 people. Word of their amazing rappings spread quickly. The Fox sisters eventually travelled to New York City and set up shop in a hotel in the financial district, where, during July and August of 1850, they conducted public and private sittings and earned 100 dollars (approximately equivalent to $2,800 today) or more a day. Later, Kate and Maggie went on tour, offering seances throughout the east coast.

The Fox sisters' time in the limelight was rather short, but they sparked a very large movement. After hearing about the 'Rochester Knockings', many people began to conduct seances in their homes, often discovering that they, too, were talented mediums. Although the Fox sisters communicated with the spirits via knocking sounds, many mediums developed more effective means of communication, including automatic writing—by which the spirit writes on paper through the medium's hand—or direct verbal communication through or with the medium. A number of alphabet 'talking boards' were also used, and in 1891 Elijah Bond received a patent for the Ouija board 'game or toy' (see Figure 6). Seances also often produced a variety of unusual psychic events, such as turning or tipping tables, levitating objects, and ghostly appearances. At a time when many people had begun to harbour religious doubts, spiritualism seemed to offer objective proof of an afterlife and the possibility of communication with departed loved ones. Particularly after the United States Civil War, and again

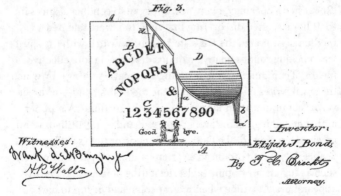

6. Drawings from the US patent application for the Ouija board 'toy or game', including a planchette and letter board.

after the First World War, the urge to make contact with lost relatives fuelled demand for the services of spiritualist mediums.

In the United States in particular, spiritualism emerged as a popular religious alternative—primarily among Protestants. Many spiritualist newspapers cropped up in cities throughout the United States, their pages filled with articles about spiritual matters and advertisements for the services of professional mediums. Perhaps the most notable of these was *The Banner of Light* published in Boston, Massachusetts, where spiritualism was particularly popular.

Part of the popularity of 19th-century spiritualism stemmed from its relationship with a number of other social movements. The Fox sisters arrived just following the second of several 'Great Awakenings' in American Protestantism—a movement that encouraged emotionalism and greater acceptance of the supernatural in an explicit reaction against the rationalism of the Enlightenment. Spiritualists found common ground with Baptists, Methodists, and Presbyterians, in the belief that anyone—not just a chosen few—could achieve salvation. In addition, these religious movements placed a great emphasis on individual purity, which fed the great social reform movements of the last half of the 19th century, including campaigns for temperance, abolitionism, women's suffrage, and child labour protections. A number of famous reformers were avid spiritualists, including Harriet Beecher Stowe, Sojourner Truth, Elizabeth Cady Stanton, Susan B. Anthony, and William Lloyd Garrison. Mary Todd Lincoln was also a spiritualist and held seances in the White House.

A common feature of both spiritualism and the social reform movements was the prominence of women in leadership roles. In the Victorian era, the home was considered the centrepiece of religious and moral life, and women were at the centre of the home. In the particular case of spiritualism, the great majority of mediums were drawn from the young women of the household. It is noteworthy that less than 100 years after the execution of Anna Göldi for the crime of witchcraft many women emerged as highly paid conjurors of spirits from another world. Indeed, the similarity to the ancient art of necromancy was not lost on spiritualism's critics. In 1873, A. B. Morrison, a pastor of the Methodist Episcopal Church, published a book called *Spiritualism and Necromancy*. Morrison did not question that mediums were in touch with spirits during their seances, but he claimed the spirits in question were demons. Such criticisms notwithstanding, spiritualism, like a number of the reform movements of the 19th century, provided new ways for women to take on leadership roles and achieve greater social and political influence.

On 31 March 1848 the Fox sisters started a movement that continued well into the 1920s, but a number of events in the late 18th century set the table for the spiritualism of the next century. One of these was Swedish engineer and mystic Emanuel Swedenborg (1688–1772), who demonstrated remarkable talents as a seer. Once, while at a dinner party with sixteen guests in Gothenburg, he claimed a fire was raging 300 miles away in Stockholm and described its progress in great detail—events that later proved to be accurate. Swedenborg reported that God had appeared to him in a dream in 1745, and in 1747 he gave up engineering and committed himself to spiritual writing. He claimed to be capable of communing with spirits in the next world, and many of his writings were about the spirit world beyond the grave.

After Swedenborg's death, interest in his writings continued to grow, and a spiritual community of Swedenborgians emerged in Europe and the United States. Once the 19th-century wave of spiritualism got under way in America, it received a warm reception from many who were followers of Swedenborg.

As we have seen, many traditional shamans, sorcerers, and magicians used various techniques to bring on a trance, and the same was true of many Victorian and early 20th-century mediums. Part of the popularity of these more modern trances came from mesmerism. The German physician Franz Mesmer (1734–1815) began a very unorthodox medical practice in 1775. Mesmer introduced the concept of *animal magnetism*, by which magnetic forces can flow through the human body and other objects. In some cases, Mesmer's methodology involved real magnets applied at various points on the body, but often magnetism was directed as a force from one person to another (see Figure 7). Mesmer began treating patients—typically women who suffered from a number of complaints—with his magnetic therapy, and his patients often went into a trance and were racked with apparently involuntary movements. Although Mesmer was

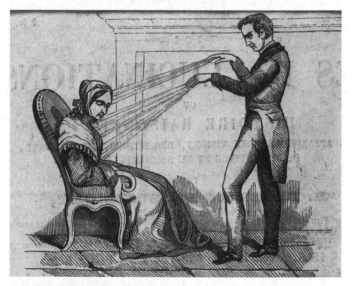

7. A practitioner using animal magnetism to mesmerize a woman who appears to go into a trance.

never accepted by the medical establishment and was dogged by a number of controversies, mesmerism, as it came to be known, drew considerable attention.

Mesmerism launched the study of hypnosis, which was taken up by the Scottish surgeon James Braid (1795–1860) and the French physician Jean-Martin Charcot (1825–93), among others, and eventually came to the attention of Sigmund Freud (1856–1939) and the American behavioural psychologist Clark Hull (1884–1952). Even today, some psychologists and psychiatrists continue to use hypnosis for the treatment of addictions, phobias, and pain management. By the time spiritualism had taken hold in the United States, trances were familiar to anyone who had heard of mesmerism. In addition, the association of mesmerism and hypnosis with the medical profession undoubtedly gave trances more credibility than they might otherwise have had.

A final important foundation for spiritualism came from Shakerism. The Shakers were a religious group that split from the Quakers of northern England in 1747. Shakers got their name from the body movements they exhibited while filled with religious feeling. During services they danced and sang, and many Shakers said they had contact with the spirit world while in a trance state. Shakerism reached its peak from 1820 to 1860, and the period from 1837 to 1850, in particular, is known as the Era of Manifestations, during which members of the Shaker communities throughout the United States—often young women—spoke in tongues and relayed communications from the 'other world'. Thus, by the time the Fox sisters arrived in 1848, the Shakers had paved the way.

Spiritualism and science

Mesmerism and spiritualism arrived when modern science was still quite young, and both played a role in the development of scientific methods of testing. Despite the objections of people like

Reverend Morrison, the Enlightenment established that the new standard for superstition would be evidence and reason, and as a result, post-Enlightenment spiritualism and science had a kind of twinned existence that was not true of earlier eras. There had always been elites who were sceptical of magicians and sorcerers, as well as of common superstitions, but for the first time, religious objections were secondary to empirical scepticism. In the case of spiritualism, the most common hypotheses were either an unconscious alliance among the participants or simple fraud, and there were many examples of both.

In the case of mesmerism, patients appeared to adopt a hypnotic role and exhibit a kind of placebo response. After a difficult start, Franz Mesmer established a very successful practice in Paris in the 1780s. Wealthy Parisians and members of the nobility became devoted followers, and the growing popularity of Mesmer's unorthodox methods raised concerns among physicians and the government. In 1784 King Louis XVI (1754–93) established a Royal Commission to investigate Mesmer, and, among others, Benjamin Franklin, America's Minister Plenipotentiary to France, was appointed to the commission. The commissioners submitted to being magnetized themselves, but, unlike Mesmer's patients, they felt nothing at all. They went on to conduct some simple experiments. The commissioners found that, when blindfolded, patients could not detect where, on their bodies, magnetization was being applied, yet when they could see, patients reported strong sensations at the correct location. In another test, when offered successive cups of water, only one of which was magnetized, patients were unable to identify the correct cup. The commission concluded that 'the imagination is the real cause of the effects attributed to magnetism'. Interestingly, once it had been established that there was no actual effect of animal magnetism, Franklin was not convinced this was sufficient reason to prohibit Mesmer's methods. As we will see, this kind of ambivalence is still seen today in response to many superstitions and placebo-like medical therapies.

Although 'imagination' was undoubtedly an important factor in the success of many spiritualist mediums, simple fraud was also rampant. On 21 October 1888, Margaret Fox (by then Margaret Fox Kane) published a signed confession in the *New York World* newspaper admitting that she and her sisters had faked the knocking noises. They had developed the ability to crack the joints in their feet with sufficient volume to be heard in a large room. Other examples of fraud were common. The magician Harry Houdini became devoted to the cause of exposing unscrupulous mediums, publishing two books on the subject of his investigations. Psychical research societies were founded in both the United States and Europe, and although most of their members were believers in the possibility of communication with spirits, they took an active role in uncovering charlatans. The American psychologist William James (1842–1910) was a founding member of the American Society for Psychical Research, and although he helped expose many fake mediums, James came to believe that one Boston medium, Mrs Leonora Piper, had genuine psychic abilities. He suffered considerable criticism from his psychology colleagues for his interest in spiritualism.

Although 19th- and early 20th-century science provided a defence against fraudulent spiritualists, new technologies supplied new avenues of deception. In 1861 William Mumler, a Boston photographer, was alone in his studio taking a self-portrait when he noticed the faint image of a young girl in the resulting print. Soon he began to advertise himself as a medium, offering sittings that produced ghostly photos (see Figure 8). Mumler was the first of many successful spirit photographers operating from the 1860s to the 1930s. Unethical practitioners easily doctored photographs to capitalize on the longings of bereaved customers.

Although the spiritualist movement largely disappeared in the 1930s, remnants of it re-emerged in the New Age movement of the 1970s and still survive today in the professional psychics, Tarot card readers, and mediums who say they are in contact with

8. Mary Todd Lincoln in a William Mumler photograph apparently showing the ghost of her husband Abraham Lincoln.

various spirits. For example, J. Z. Knight is an American medium who claims to channel the spirit of Ramtha, a warrior from Lemuria, a hypothetical 'lost land', who lived 35,000 years ago. Ramtha speaks through Knight in modern English.

Superstition today

Up to this point we have followed the bending path of the word superstition as it was applied to various foreign religions and unauthorized systems of belief, but having arrived at the Age of Science, it is time to establish a definition for superstition today. Although, as the saying goes, 'It is difficult to make predictions, especially about the future', science is likely to be the standard for all natural phenomena for the foreseeable future. There will always be some people who—like creationists—look to religious texts rather than science for their understanding of the natural world, but the evidence suggests that science—not religion—provides our clearest understanding of the universe. As a result, today the word superstition means 'bad science', rather than bad religion.

What superstition isn't

Although the standards we use to identify a superstition have changed, it is desirable that our modern definition flow from prior usage in some coherent way, and a good place to start might be to identify a few things superstition is not.

A blunt object. In 1994, Paul R. Gross and Norman Levitt published *Higher Superstition: The Academic Left and its Quarrels with Science*. Although their book was about what they considered to be a dangerous rejection of science and Enlightenment thinking among liberals in academia, Gross and Levitt were not using the word superstition in a way that is useful to us. In the everyday world of political dialogue and media commentary, the word superstition is hurled like a brickbat at any unsupported idea. In these instances, it is merely a synonym for ignorant, outdated, unsophisticated, or any number of other pejorative adjectives. People are likely to continue to use the word in this way, but if our definition is to be meaningful, it must be much narrower.

Religion. As we have seen, for most of its history the word superstition has been used to describe rival religious practices, and, as a result, it might seem fitting that a modern definition would simply encompass all religious practice. Indeed, much of the thrust of Enlightenment thinking moved in this direction. For example, in an essay called 'Of Superstition and Enthusiasm', Scottish philosopher David Hume (1711–76) used these terms to describe 'two species of false religion'. Superstition was characterized by fearful practices to appease the dreaded unknown agents assumed to control the world, including 'ceremonies, observances, mortifications, sacrifices, presents or in any practice, however absurd or frivolous, which either folly or knavery recommends to a blind and terrified credulity'. According to Hume, superstitious people were drawn to priestly intermediators—an obvious reference to Catholics. In contrast, Hume's term enthusiasm referred to those who felt they could experience the divine directly, and, in this case, he pointed to Shakers as an example. Taken together Hume's two species of false religion incorporated many of the popular faiths of his time. Similarly, the French writer Voltaire used the term superstition to describe a kind of religious fanaticism that he saw throughout Europe and that, in his view, encouraged sectarian hatred: 'superstition sets the world on fire; philosophy puts out the flames'. Voltaire was an avid deist and Hume's religious beliefs are unclear, but unlike the earlier Protestant attacks on Catholic ritual, these Enlightenment indictments of religious superstition applied more broadly to many faiths. Later philosophers, including Friedrich Nietzsche (1844–1900) and Albert Camus (1913–60) would be much more explicitly atheist.

Today's atheist writers tend not to use religion and superstition interchangeably. Of the 'Four Horsemen' of the new atheist movement—Richard Dawkins, Daniel Dennett, Sam Harris, and Christopher Hitchens—Harris has come the closest to calling religion a superstition. In a 2005 blog post entitled 'An Atheist Manifesto', he referred to 'Southern and Midwestern states, characterized by the highest levels of religious superstition and hostility to evolutionary theory'. But to the extent that atheist writers utter both words in the same breath, they seem to be using superstition as a blunt object. They offer no direct analysis of how religion might be understood to be a superstition.

Given that superstition—and not religion—is our concern, I think it is easy to make a useful distinction between the two. As I will discuss more fully below, superstitions tend to be much more narrowly pragmatic than religious practice. The religious person pursues their observance for a variety of reasons. Praying, attending services, and celebrating holidays are rarely motivated by a single desired outcome. Superstitions, on the other hand, are typically aimed at a current need. As we will see, there are points of overlap. Some individual activities or observances based in religion can be accurately called superstitious, but to say religion in general or any individual faith is a superstition is just one more blunt use of the term.

Mental illness. A number of mental disorders involve irrational thinking, but the condition that most closely resembles superstition is obsessive compulsive disorder (OCD). OCD is an anxiety disorder that involves obsessive thoughts and compulsive actions. Some sufferers obsess about germs and wash their hands repeatedly. Others are compulsive checkers, inspecting the stove over and over again to make sure the oven and burners are turned off. This kind of behaviour bears an obvious similarity to Theophrastus' Superstitious Man who washes himself in three springs before going out for the day, and, as a result, it would be a reasonable assumption that the two are related. Perhaps superstition is on a continuum with OCD such that too much superstition leads to mental illness.

The available psychology research does not support this conclusion. For example, early childhood superstitions do not predict the later development of OCD. In addition, mental disorders usually cause problems in some area of the individual's life, and although they are based in irrational thinking, the overwhelming majority of everyday superstitions do not produce the kind of suffering associated with OCD and other psychiatric conditions. Finally, as we will see in Chapter 5, a number of surveys show that superstition is widespread; whereas mental disorders are typically rare. By labelling something as common as superstition a mental disorder we would be turning a part of normal human behaviour into a disease.

What superstition is

A number of definitions of superstition have been offered, but the following has the benefit of simplicity.

Inconsistent with science. Superstitions typically lack evidence to support their effectiveness, and, in addition, their presumed mechanism of action is inconsistent with our understanding of the physical world. We have no evidence that a different world exists where the spirits of the dead live and talk. Similarly, concepts of luck that portray it as a force that can come and go—or a quality that some people have and others don't—do not conform to what we know about physics and human behaviour.

Instrumental or pragmatic. Some beliefs are non-scientific but have no practical implications for us. Many people believe in ghosts or in the possibility of extrasensory perception (ESP), but unless you are attempting to harness your ESP to play the stock market or win at the race track, your belief is merely paranormal, not superstitious. Superstitions are the subset of paranormal beliefs that are purported to have practical uses.

This can be an important distinction. For example, it is clear that the seances of the 19th and early 20th centuries were often a form of evening entertainment, but many people paid considerable sums of money in the hope of making contact with a dead friend or relative. Going to a seance or psychic for fun, much as one might attend a magic show, does not fit our definition of superstition. Going to a seance or psychic as a means of learning about future events or communicating with a dead loved one does.

Culturally fair. Because it is something of an epithet, it is important to impose some limits on the use of the term. If a culture has not yet adopted science as its standard, then what we consider magic or superstition is more accurately the local science or religion. Just as, in hindsight, it was illogical for the adherents of one religion to label similar beliefs in another religion superstitious, it is unfair to classify the beliefs of a pre-scientific culture as superstitious. Similarly, children often subscribe to a variety of magical beliefs, but until they are educated in the standards of evidence, we should avoid giving them pejorative labels.

This definition provides a useful framework for the kinds of superstitions that inhabit our modern world, but in order to get a better grip on the subject, it helps to classify superstitions into topographical categories. Fortunately, the psychologist Gustav Jahoda established four types of superstitions that describe the territory well.

Superstitions forming part of a cosmology or world-view. Many basic religious beliefs are not amenable to scientific testing and are, by definition, taken on faith—or not. But other religious claims are about the natural world and, as a result, appropriate topics for science. When these claims fail the test, they should be considered superstitions. For example, if anyone still adheres to the belief that holy water or consecrated candle wax has special protective powers, these suggestions could easily be tested. Many people believe in faith healing, but the existing systematic evaluations do not support its effectiveness. Faith healing, though based in religion, should be considered a superstition. Finally, if we consider the deterministic framework of astrology to be a kind of cosmology, then it would fit into this category. If, like President Reagan, you use an astrologer to help you make decisions about what you should do, that is a superstition.

Other socially shared superstitions. This category includes the superstitions that we learn simply as a function of growing up within a culture, such as the fear of black cats or the number 13, as well as the belief that four-leaf clovers are lucky. Much of the remainder of this chapter will be devoted to a short catalogue of these superstitions.

Occult experiences of individuals. This category would include many paranormal phenomena, such as belief in ghosts or ESP, that we are not calling superstitions, as well as some instrumental acts that we are. If you go to a medium to be guided or comforted by communications from beyond the grave, then your actions would be superstitious.

Personal superstitions. Finally, many everyday superstitions are ones we discover through personal experience and adopt as our own. The model Heidi Klum is said to carry a bag of her own baby teeth with her at all times for luck, and the singer Taylor Swift, who was born on 13 December, considers the number lucky for her. She turned 13 on Friday the 13th; her Twitter handle is @taylorswift13; and she sometimes paints the number 13 on the back of her hand. Former Boston Red Sox third baseman Wade Boggs believed that eating chicken made him hit better, so he ate chicken before every game of his major league career. Because personal superstitions are unique to the individual, they get less attention than the more familiar socially shared superstitions, but they are very common.

A brief catalogue of popular superstitions and their origins

In a little book like this one it is impossible to provide a complete accounting of popular superstitions in any one geographical location, much less the world at large. For example, in 1984 Anthon Cannon and colleagues published a collection of 13,207 superstitions and folk beliefs indigenous to the US state of Utah alone. Instead, I will describe some of the most popular superstitions worldwide and their presumed sources. As we will see, in some cases, very venerable and familiar superstitions have somewhat unclear origins. When we try to establish where a superstition comes from, we must look backward into a murky and largely unrecorded history of folk beliefs, and often history provides only a fuzzy image. If your favourite superstition is not here, I have listed a number of dictionaries and encyclopedias of superstition in the Further reading section.

Number superstitions

13. Fear of the number 13, sometimes rather pretentiously called *triskaidekaphobia*, is arguably the most famous of all superstitions but also the most hotly debated. There are three main theories about its origin and several minor ones, and whenever I am quoted in the media offering what I believe to be the best account, I receive angry emails from defenders of the others. The credit for nailing down this particular controversy—at least in my mind—goes to Nathaniel Lachenmeyer, who did extensive archival research for his book *13: The Story of the World's Most Popular Superstition*.

We have already encountered one of the competing theories. The Knights Templar were arrested on Friday, 13 October 1307, and eventually many of them, including their leader Jacques de Molay,

72

were burned at the stake. Many people subscribe to this theory of the origin of Friday the 13th, including Ari Lehman who, as a child actor in the first instalment of the series, played the role of Jason Vorhees, the murderous antagonist of the *Friday the 13th* horror movie franchise.

The other popular competing theory is drawn from Norse mythology. According to legend a group of twelve Norse gods were relaxing in Valhalla when they were joined by the evil god Loki who fashioned a plan that resulted in the death of the beloved god Baldur. Thus, according to this theory, a group of thirteen people is unlucky.

The theory that has the most evidence to back it up involves a different group of thirteen people: the participants in the biblical Last Supper. According to the standard account, the Last Supper was attended by Jesus and his twelve disciples, one of whom, Judas Iscariot, betrayed Jesus, leading to the Crucifixion the next day. As a result, the first version of the thirteen superstition proposed that sitting thirteen at a table will lead to the death of one of the group by the end of the year.

Lachenmeyer dismisses the Knights Templar theory as he found no mention of the Friday the 13th superstition before 1913, seven centuries after the Knights' arrest. In the case of the death of Baldur theory, Lachenmeyer found that, according to the earliest authoritative account of the legend, Loki's arrival at Valhalla produced a total of fourteen gods, not thirteen. Finally, Lachenmeyer's research turned up no mentions of the thirteen superstition until the 17th century in England. At the end of the 17th century he found two different references to unlucky thirteen published fifteen years apart, each of which described the taboo of thirteen people at a table.

The superstition about thirteen at a table continued into the 19th century, and in 1881 Captain William Fowler, an eccentric Civil War veteran, founded the first of several Thirteen Clubs in

New York City. This unusual social club held its meetings on the thirteenth day of each month in room 13 of the building Fowler bought for the purpose. During their meetings members would join in groups of thirteen, sit around a table, and eat dinner. Fowler was quite a promoter, and he managed to get five US presidents to accept honorary memberships to the club. Other Thirteen clubs sprang up in London and Philadelphia.

Independently, Friday was considered unlucky because the Crucifixion had happened on a Friday and because hangings were traditionally conducted on Fridays. Interestingly, quite separate from their efforts to demystify the number thirteen, the members of New York's Thirteen Club advocated policies that would destroy the fear of Fridays. They were vocal supporters of making Saturday a full day holiday for most workers, a standard that eventually made Friday a very happy day ('Thank God It's Friday'), and they publicly praised judges who scheduled executions on days other than Friday.

Friday the 13th as a specific fearful date was not launched until the early 20th century. Lachenmeyer found a few prior mentions of the ominous co-occurrence of Good Friday on the thirteenth day of the month, but as a mathematical necessity this happened very rarely. But in 1907 the Boston financier Thomas W. Lawson published a novel called *Friday, the Thirteenth*, in which a stock trader attempted to manipulate the market on Friday the 13th. Lawson advertised the book extensively, particularly in September of that year, when the thirteenth day of the month fell on Friday. Additional publicity came his way when a man was arrested for attempting to manipulate the Philadelphia stock market using the theory presented in Lawson's novel. Lachenmeyer argues that Lawson's novel and the subsequent 1916 movie version (now lost to history) established the idea that Friday the 13th was a particularly unlucky day.

Today the simple idea that thirteen is unlucky and the companion superstition that Friday the 13th is particularly unlucky have all but blotted out the concept of a group of thirteen people. However, some years ago, I was at a cocktail party where a professor said he was taking a group of twelve students on a trip abroad, and in what appeared to be all seriousness, the person next to me said, 'Well, you'd better recruit another student.' Later it occurred to me, 12 (students) + 1 (professor) = 13. But other worries about the number thirteen are still very common. Elevator panels for tall buildings often do not provide a button for the thirteenth floor (in which case, we all understand that it is incorrectly labelled fourteen), and airport departure gates are very rarely numbered 13 (see Figure 9).

3. There is wide agreement that three is a magical number, but its influence can be good or bad. The third time is often considered to be 'the charm'. If at first you don't succeed, try, try again. The idea of three being a perfect number comes from Pythagoras' magical ideas about the equilateral triangle and from the Christian holy trinity. But bad things are also said to happen in threes.

One of the most interesting three superstitions is the idea that lighting three cigarettes on a match is unlucky. The origins of this superstition are debated, but the most common theory suggests it derives from a wartime precaution of either the Crimean War or the First World War. In theory, soldiers who kept a match lit too long on the battlefield at night could attract a sniper's fire, and as a result, lighting three cigarettes on a single match became a taboo that spread far beyond the trenches. At the beginning of the 1932 film *Three on a Match*, friends played by Joan Blondell, Ann Dvorak, and Bette Davis light three cigarettes on a single match and discuss the superstition. As you can imagine, things soon take a turn for the worse.

4, 14, and **8.** Numbers are everywhere. They are associated with dates, sums of money, ages, theatre tickets, and airport departure gates. They pop up all the time in random places.

9. Elevator panel from a Las Vegas hotel. The thirteenth floor is missing.

They also are spoken words, and sometimes objects acquire special qualities due to random associations. In Chinese the number 4 (四) sounds similar to 死 (sǐ), which means 'death', and as a result 4 is sometimes believed to be an unlucky number, as are numbers containing fours, such as 14. In contrast, the number 8 八 sounds like 發 (fa), which means 'fortune' and 'prosper'. Lucky and unlucky numbers often show up in the marketplace, and studies have shown that Chinese products are priced with lucky and unlucky numbers in mind. Eights are substantially overrepresented, and fours are rare. In 2003, Sichuan Airlines paid the equivalent of $280,000 to obtain a phone number made up of eight eights, 88888888.

17. Similarly, the number seventeen is unlucky in Italy because the Roman numeral XVII can be rearranged to spell VIXI, which in Latin translates to 'I have lived', or alternatively, 'My life is over' or 'I have died'. These examples show how random associations can adhere to numbers, making them lucky or unlucky.

18. Jewish Kabbalistic numerology translates names and written words into numbers to reveal another layer of meaning. The Hebrew word chai, חי, means 'life', and its gematria or number equivalent is 18. Chai has a special luck-enhancing role in Jewish culture. Many people wear jewellery with the חי symbol on it, and the word is part of the traditional toast L'chaim!, 'To life!' The American baseball player Rod Carew wore a chai necklace on the field, and Wade Boggs drew a חי in the dirt of the batting box with his bat before stepping up to the plate. It is a traditional Jewish practice to give bar or bat mitzvah gifts or charitable contributions in multiples of eighteen.

7. There are several explanations for why seven should be a lucky number. Often this is tied to the Babylonian decision to establish a calendar with a seven-day week linked to the seven known planets of that time. Some of our current days of the week retain their planetary appellations, including Saturday (Saturn), Sunday, and Monday (Moon). In addition, according to the Book of Genesis, the world was created in seven days. Finally, the gematria for the Hebrew word for luck, gad גָּד, is 7, and mazal מַזָּל, another word for luck, translates to 77.

The colours of things

Black cats. The notion that black cats are unlucky or that it is unlucky for a black cat to cross your path is a remnant of the European era of witchcraft paranoia. Witches consorted with black cats, and shapeshifting witches could turn themselves into cats. Thus, the cat you met on the path might actually be a witch.

Red wedding dresses. In Chinese culture, the colour red is associated with prosperity and good fortune. Marketers often offer red coloured products, and Chinese brides traditionally wear a red wedding dress for luck. Their dresses are often decorated with gold dragons and phoenixes, which are also thought to be good luck.

Something blue. Superstitions are often associated with big events that people hope will go well, such as weddings, the birth of a child, or the start of a new year. In the west the most common wedding superstition is that the bride should wear:

> Something old,
> Something new,
> Something borrowed,
> Something blue.

The verses have been traced to 19th-century Lancashire in England, and an older version includes a final line, 'And a silver sixpence in her shoe.' Although the inclusion of 'something blue' may simply have been for want of a rhyme, the colour blue is thought to be a symbol of fidelity.

Other traditional western superstitions

Walking under ladders. Some superstitions once had a rational basis that no longer applies. For example, the theatre taboo about not whistling backstage derives from a time when scenery was raised and lowered by a crew that manoeuvred ropes and pulleys. These stage workers, who were often former sailors, signalled to each other by whistling. So, the actor who whistled backstage might get a piece of scenery dropped on their head.

Similarly, I have always felt that avoiding ladders was somewhat rational, particularly if someone is on the ladder as you walk beneath it. And even when unoccupied, ladders are not always the sturdiest of constructions. However, the most often cited source of this superstition is religious. The triangle shape was once thought to be symbolic of the holy trinity, and violating it by walking under the ladder was a blasphemous act that would bring bad luck.

Breaking a mirror. Before mirrors became widely available, they were very valuable and somewhat mysterious. Magicians used looking glasses in a visual form of divination, like gazing into a crystal ball, and there are many legends about things not appearing in a mirror as they do in the real world. In Bram Stoker's 1897 novel *Dracula*, the vampire's image was not reflected in a looking glass. Even today, Jews cover all the mirrors in a house for the seven days that a family is in mourning. According to Kabbalists, one reason for this practice is that demons attempt to prey on a family in mourning, and although these spirits are not normally visible, they can be seen in a mirror.

Given all these special qualities surrounding mirrors, it is not unusual that breaking a mirror became a taboo. It is not clear why the notion of seven years of bad luck should adhere to this mishap, but it has been part of the legend at least since the 19th century in England. Prior to that, it was often said that someone in the family would die in the next year.

Spilling salt. Salt has long been a highly valued condiment and food preservative. As we have seen in Chapter 3, blessed salt was used for many purposes in Europe of the Middle Ages and Renaissance, and it is still a sacramental that is used as part of Anglican and Catholic baptism ceremonies. Even today some people still believe that consecrated salt is capable of keeping demons away. Blessed sea salt from the Dead Sea can be purchased on the Internet, and purchasers use it to bless any number of objects or events.

It is easy to imagine why spilling such a valuable substance would be considered bad luck. Less obvious is the origin of the common countermeasure of tossing some of the spilled salt over your left shoulder. The most common explanation was to ward off the devil, who—being a devil—was most likely to come at you from the left and behind.

Four-leaf clovers. A long-standing legend, most often associated with Ireland, suggests that finding a four-leaf clover is a sign of luck. The origin of this superstition seems to come from the simple fact that three-leaf clovers are the overwhelming norm, and four-leaf clovers are quite rare. So, by definition, the person who finds a four-leaf clover is lucky to have done so. However, the common idea of luck as a quality that can adhere to this small green thing—or more generally as a force that can come and go—is non-scientific.

Crossing fingers and knocking on wood. These two gestures are somewhat special because, unlike most other superstitions, they are often done in public. When we want something good to happen—or something bad *not* to happen—crossing fingers or knocking on wood is an expression of a shared hope. Crossed fingers are an invocation of the Christian cross. The origin of knocking on wood is unclear but may derive from an ancient belief in tree spirits.

Horseshoes. Horseshoes have long been purported to be a valuable adornment to buildings, often nailed above the front door, both to ward off bad luck and to bring good. Lord Horatio Nelson was said to have nailed one to the mast of HMS *Victory* to protect all aboard. Knowing my interest in superstition, a student once brought me a horseshoe which I proudly hung on the wall of my office.

There are many explanations offered for the horseshoe superstition. One popular story involves St Dunstan, Archbishop of Canterbury (*c.*909–88 CE), who, as a young man, worked as a blacksmith. According to legend, a two-legged creature with hooves approached wanting to be shod, but Dunstan recognized him as the devil and pounded the nails in so deeply that the animal ran away in pain vowing never again to enter a building with a horseshoe over the door. Another theory suggests that witches were afraid of horses—which explained why they flew around on broomsticks—and, as a result, would avoid a house marked with a horseshoe. As my student was quick to tell me, horseshoes are typically mounted with the opening of the shoe pointing up in a U-shape—else the luck will fall out.

More elaborate systems of superstition

Up to this point most of the superstitions we have encountered in this brief catalogue have been relatively discrete. A number of them are related to religious practices, but they are simple superstitions. The following examples have many more pieces, and in some cases, they are extensive enough to fit into Jahoda's category of superstitions forming part of a cosmology or world-view.

The evil eye. The evil eye superstition has a long history dating back at least to 7th-century-BCE Akkadian and Assyrian literature. In *The Natural History*, Pliny the Elder mentioned Balkan tribes who 'have the power of fascination with the eyes, and can even kill those on whom they fix their gaze for any length of time', and today the evil eye is a familiar belief in wide swathes of Europe, the Middle East, south Asia, and South America.

The particulars of the evil eye superstition vary widely by culture, but there are a few common elements. First, it is based on the idea that some people have the power to harm you merely by looking—by wielding the evil eye in your direction. Typically, the motivation for the attack is covetousness. The victim has something of great value—babies are a common target—and the attacker wants to harm the person—or the baby—out of envy. In other cases, the evil eye is blamed for an illness. Often the worry seems to be that a person who is very fortunate is also vulnerable to loss, and being too complimentary about a baby or another person increases the risk of attracting the evil eye.

The countermeasure for the evil eye is distraction. In south Asia, it is common for parents to paint a black dot on a baby's forehead or cheek as a target to attract the eye away from the child. Similarly, there is a brisk market for charms and necklaces to protect against the evil eye. Often these items have the shape of an eye incorporated into their design, and it is thought that these talismans have the power to turn the evil eye back on the perpetrator. The Turkish blue and white glass *nazar* are very popular as necklaces or to be hung in the home (see Figure 10). Similarly, the hand-shaped *hamsa*, which is said to be a protection against the evil eye, often includes the image of an eye in the palm of the hand. In Italian culture, a horn-shaped pendant is used for protection (see Figure 11).

In Italy it is common to blame the evil eye, which is known as *malocchio*, whenever anyone is ill or has a headache. To determine whether the illness is due to the evil eye or just normal disease, the believer may engage in a divination process that typically involves placing several drops of olive oil into a small bowl of water and saying several prayers. If the oil appears in the water as separate drops, there is no *malocchio* present, but if the oil appears as

10. A glass Turkish *nazar*.

11. A horn charm used to ward off *malocchio*.

runny streams, then the illness is caused by *malocchio*. Often, if *malocchio* is blamed, then salt and additional prayers are used to remove the curse.

Astrology. As we have seen, astrology is an ancient form of divination that was thought to have originated in Babylonia 4,000 years ago and eventually spread throughout Asia and Europe. The Mayans are also thought to have had their own system of astrology. With a history that far outstrips most of the world's great religions, astrology is a remarkable success story. The simple western sun sign form of astrology ('What's your sign?') is arguably the most popular theory of personality in the world.

The western form of astrology is based on the theory that the position of the stars and planets at the time of your birth determines your personality. The twelve constellations that make up the zodiac identify twelve sun signs. More elaborate personalized astrological charts can be drawn up for you by an astrologer, a computer program, or a website. The Chinese astrology system uses twelve animals associated with your birth year according to the Chinese calendar, and Jyotisha or Hindu Vedic astrology uses a zodiac similar to but slightly different from the western zodiac.

Unfortunately for its many adherents, science has not been kind to astrology. Numerous research studies using validated measures of personality have failed to find any connection between personality traits and birthdates. In addition, when presented with personality descriptions based on their own and another person's astrological chart, people cannot identify their own chart at better than chance levels. So, belief in astrology qualifies as a superstition under our definition. Of course, many people visit psychics, astrologers, and Tarot card readers merely as a form of entertainment, but, if you believe in astrology—and especially if you rely on astrology for advice on personal or business decisions—you are engaging in a modern superstition.

Homeopathy. In Europe, the USA, and many other places in the world, homeopathic medicines are very popular. Homeopathy was developed by German physician Samuel Christian Hahnemann (1755–1843), who based it on two primary principles. The first was 'like cures like': a disease can be cured by a herb or substance that produces the same symptoms as the disease in a healthy person. The second principle was that homeopathic medicines were more effective if they were highly diluted, an idea that turns all homeopathic medicines into placebos. Homeopathic medicines are often so highly diluted that the substances they are purported to contain are no longer detectable—which is sometimes a very good thing. Belladonna, a highly poisonous substance drawn from the deadly nightshade plant, was endorsed as a homeopathic medicine by Hahnemann and is still promoted for the treatment of colds and flu.

The success of homeopathy can be explained in part by the nature of its competitors. Homeopathy was launched in Europe in the early 19th century and arrived in the USA in 1825. At that time, establishment medical practice was still based on the theory that diseases were caused by imbalances of the four humours: phlegm, blood, black bile, and yellow bile. Restoring the balance of humours involved using a number of practices that fell under the label *heroic medicine*—a fitting description given that patients had to be rather heroic to endure them. Standard therapies included purges that induced vomiting or diarrhoea, and other medicines that induced fever and sweating. The most popular and dangerous of all heroic treatments was bloodletting. The esteemed American physician and signer of the Declaration of Independence, Benjamin Rush (1746–1813), was a particularly strong proponent of bloodletting, which undoubtedly hastened the death of many of his patients.

This was the state of medicine when homeopathy arrived, and it is easy to see why a harmless placebo therapy would be more appealing than heroic medicine. Evolution has supplied *Homo sapiens* with many natural defences, and placebos can have very powerful effects. For example, research shows that a substantial part of the effect of anti-depression medications is due to the placebo effect. The 19th century saw the introduction of a number of other relatively benign therapies that, in combination with homeopathy, helped bring about the demise of heroic medicine, and homeopathic medicine achieved such a following that these treatments have survived as popular over-the-counter remedies at local drug and health food stores.

Like astrology, homeopathy is a form of pseudoscience. It has some of the trappings of a science and is based on a crazy kind of logic, but it is inconsistent with known principles of pharmacology. More importantly, research has failed to find any effect of these therapies beyond what would be expected from a placebo. So, any benefit it draws from the appearance of being based in science is unearned, and belief in and use of homeopathic treatments is a form of superstition.

Feng shui. Feng shui is a Chinese form of geomancy—divination based on land formations and markings. The words 'feng shui' mean 'wind and water', and it is thought that living in harmony with the winds and waters of the Earth promotes happiness and prosperity. As a result, believers hire feng shui consultants to advise them on the construction and decoration of homes, offices, and public spaces to maximize the flow of positive Qi, the life force that is also a basic concept in traditional Chinese medicine. Feng shui has roots in ancient Taoism and is deeply embedded in Chinese history and culture, but after the founding of the People's Republic of China in 1949, the government labelled feng shui superstitious and waged a harsh crackdown on practitioners. The attitude toward feng shui is slightly more tolerant today, but feng shui remains substantially less popular in mainland China than it is in Hong Kong, Taiwan, and Singapore. The overwhelming majority of home buyers in Hong Kong consult a feng shui master before making a purchase. But the appeal of feng shui extends far beyond Asia. There are many feng shui consultants in Europe, the UK, and the USA.

As you may have anticipated, there is no scientific support for feng shui. In fact, there is no evidence that Qi is a real thing. So, feng shui represents a very popular superstition.

These are just a few of the many socially shared superstitions in our contemporary world. InChapter 5 we will turn to a discussion of personal superstitions and the important question, Why do people believe?

Chapter 5

The psychology of superstition

The inquisitions and witch trials are over. There are still a surprising number of places in Asia, Africa, Europe, and the Middle East where people can be fined, jailed, or even executed for expressing the wrong religious views, but, in most of the world, what we now call superstition qualifies you for a little teasing at worst. Nonetheless, holding superstitious beliefs in a time when the fruits of science are all around us seems somewhat paradoxical. In the pre-Enlightenment world of superstition, the challenging and often disputed task was to draw a line separating permitted beliefs from forbidden ones. Now that science is the dominant standard, the line is drawn between ways of thinking that are closer to being categorically different. As a result, it should be easier for modern people to find the borderlines between superstition and science, and yet many people cross those borders every day. Furthermore, as we will see, there are a few places—even today—where the lines are blurred.

The prevalence and demographics of superstitious belief

Before we attempt to determine why people are superstitious, we might ask ourselves how big is this phenomenon? How many people are superstitious and what are they superstitious about? There are a number of ways we can get a handle on this question, and one of the best is public opinion research. Surveys are expensive to conduct, and as interesting as superstition may be to us, opinion researchers do not turn to this topic very often. However, there are some data we can draw upon.

Prevalence. In October of 2017, as Friday the 13th was approaching, OnePoll.com conducted a survey of UK adults. They found that 22 per cent of respondents were worried about what would happen on Friday the 13th. In addition, 70 per cent would not risk walking under a ladder; 52 per cent believed in luck; and overall, 55 per cent considered themselves to be superstitious.

A decade earlier, the market research firm Ipsos MORI teamed up with Ben Schott of *Schott's Almanac* to survey UK adults about a range of beliefs, some of which fit our definition of superstition. A selection of those results is presented in Figure 12. Note that only 22 per cent of the sample considered themselves to be superstitious, many fewer than in the 2017 OnePoll.com study. Since the surveys were conducted by different firms, we should not conclude that superstitious belief shot up in the decade between 2007 and 2017, but the Ipsos MORI survey showed that many British adults endorsed a variety of popular superstitions.

In the UK, a common nursery rhyme about magpies reinforces the belief that seeing a single bird is unlucky. The 'One for Sorrow' nursery rhyme is several centuries old and has been handed down in various forms, but a popular modern version goes like this:

> One for sorrow,
> Two for joy,
> Three for a girl,
> Four for a boy,
> Five for silver,
> Six for gold,
> Seven for a secret,
> Never to be told.

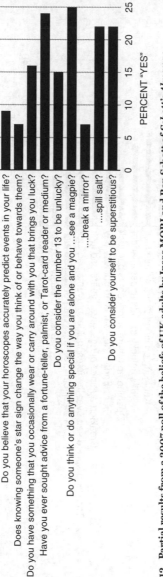

Do you believe that your horoscopes accurately predict events in your life?
Does knowing someone's star sign change the way you think of or behave towards them?
Do you have something that you occasionally wear or carry around with you that brings you luck?
Have you ever sought advice from a fortune-teller, palmist, or Tarot-card reader or medium?
Do you consider the number 13 to be unlucky?
Do you think or do anything special if you are alone and you ....see a magpie?
....break a mirror?
....spill salt?
Do you consider yourself to be superstitious?

PERCENT "YES"

12. Partial results from a 2007 poll of the beliefs of UK adults by Ipsos MORI and Ben Schott of *Schott's Almanac*.

Superstition

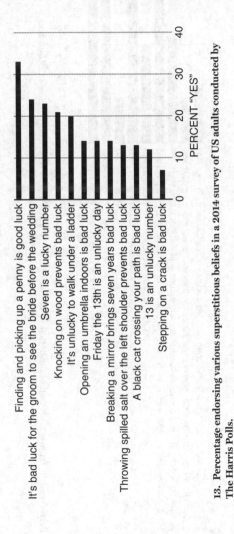

13. Percentage endorsing various superstitious beliefs in a 2014 survey of US adults conducted by The Harris Polls.

According to legend, greeting the bird with the phrase, 'Good morning, Mr Magpie. How is your lady wife today?' is an effective countermeasure against bad luck, but some people cross themselves or employ some other ritual. Approximately 25 per cent of respondents said they 'thought or did something' if they were alone and saw a single magpie. Doing something after spilling salt—most likely tossing a bit of it over their left shoulder—was also quite common, with 22 per cent of respondents admitting to this. In addition, 9 per cent of people reported their horoscopes accurately predicted the future, and a remarkable 24 per cent of people said they had 'sought advice from a fortune-teller, palmist, or Tarot-card reader or medium'. After coming through the previous chapters, we may think of shamans, sorcerers, and augurs as things from the past, but it is clear they still enjoy a substantial customer base.

A 2014 Harris poll of US adults asked about their endorsement of a variety of superstitions (see Figure 13). Americans reported the highest support for the idea that finding a penny was good luck (33 per cent) and the lowest for stepping on a crack being bad luck (7 per cent). A 2007 USA Today/Gallup poll of American adults found that 13 per cent (!) would be uncomfortable if they were assigned a hotel room on the 13th floor, and 9 per cent of the sample said they would be sufficiently bothered to ask for a different room.

Demographics

Gender. Belief in superstition has a fairly consistent demographic picture that is borne out in these polls. First, women are a bit more superstitious than men. Prior studies have shown that men are more likely to believe in Unidentified Flying Objects (UFOs) and unusual life forms, such as Big Foot; however, for most conventional superstitions, women are more likely to believe than men. In the OnePoll.com survey, UK women were more concerned about the coming Friday the 13th than men, 26 per cent to

17 per cent. If placed on the thirteenth floor of a hotel, 14 per cent of US women in the Gallup study said they would ask for a different room, compared to only 5 per cent of men. Finally, in the Harris poll, 37 per cent of US women agreed that finding a penny was good luck, compared to 29 per cent of men. It is not entirely clear where these gender differences come from. One hypothesis is that women are still socialized differently from men, and belief in superstition is more likely to be part of the acculturation process for women than for men.

British psychologists Richard Wiseman and Caroline Watt made an important contribution when they recognized that some superstitions are hopeful and positive (e.g. four-leaf clovers) and others are negative and fear-based (e.g. the number 13). This distinction had been largely overlooked by previous researchers. Wiseman and Watt found evidence that people endorse positive superstitions more than negative ones, but they also found that the typical gender difference—women being more superstitious than men—was especially true for positive superstitions and almost disappeared for negative ones.

Age. Another consistent trend shows that younger adults tend to be more superstitious than older people. In the OnePoll.com survey, two-thirds of UK adults who were 18 to 24 years old considered themselves superstitious as compared to 53 per cent of people 55 and older. The Harris poll of US adults shows a smooth trend of decreasing belief in most superstitions with increasing age. For example, belief that Friday the 13th was unlucky was 19 per cent for 18–35-year-olds, 14 per cent for 37–48-year-olds, 12 per cent for 49–67-year-olds, and only 8 per cent for people 65 and older. One might imagine these figures represent a generational effect and there is something about the experiences of today's millennials that makes them more superstitious than their elders, but this finding has been so consistent over so many studies that it is more likely we become sceptical as we age.

Politics. In the United States there is a suggestion that liberals are more superstitious than conservatives. In the Harris poll, Democrats were more likely to believe that seven is a lucky number (28 per cent) than either Republicans (20 per cent) or Independents (20 per cent).

I should point out that polling data like these are limited in a number of ways. First, people are often embarrassed about their superstitions. With the notable exceptions of crossing fingers and knocking on wood, most people are reluctant to perform their superstitions in the presence of others, and they are shy about admitting they are superstitious. The OnePoll.com researchers partially accounted for this by asking what respondents would do 'if alone' when they saw a magpie, broke a mirror, or spilled salt. This reluctance to embrace one's superstitions probably applies even when filling out an anonymous questionnaire, and, as a result, there is a good chance the figures in these surveys underestimate the true levels of belief.

Belief in luck

People who employ superstitions often say they are trying to bring good luck or avoid bad, and a number of the familiar superstitions are described in these terms. In Chinese culture, the colour red and the number eight are said to be lucky. In the West, the number thirteen is unlucky. Some objects are described as lucky charms or talismans (e.g. four-leaf clovers and horseshoes). But those who accept these descriptions are expressing an implicit theory of luck and circumstance.

Some people don't believe in luck at all. If you take a rational, scientific approach, then things happen just when and how they are supposed to according to the forces of nature. But for those who believe in luck, there are several ways to think about it. For example, some people believe they are blessed with good luck as a general quality. Things just seem to go their way. Others believe the opposite—that they are generally unlucky. Research shows that, for people who believe in it, luck is an idea that is different from a general optimism or a sense of satisfaction with life circumstances.

In addition to luck as a stable trait, some people's theory of luck includes the idea that they can do things to improve or diminish their luck. Finally, research has produced the not particularly surprising finding that belief in any of these forms of luck—stable good, stable bad, and changeable—is correlated with belief in superstition. So, luck and superstition go hand in hand.

Superstition and personality

Psychological researchers spend quite a bit of time trying to figure out how people's personalities differ from one another and the various implications of being introverted or extraverted, open to new experiences or set in our ways, as well as many other characteristics. To study these dimensions, researchers have designed questionnaires that ask participants about their beliefs, attitudes, and behaviours. There are many well-researched questionnaires or 'scales' to measure important personality traits, and, as it turns out, some of them measure the degree of belief in superstition. As we will see, the available research shows that being superstitious is correlated with a number of personality dimensions that are, in most cases, not particularly desirable.

Stress and anxiety. During the First World War, the Polish anthropologist Bronislaw Malinowski studied and lived in the Trobriand Islands, which are now part of Papua New Guinea. The Trobriand people of Malinowski's time had a well-developed understanding of farming and many other things, but they also employed magicians to help ensure a good crop. They were active fishing people, and Malinowski noticed that their magical practices were sensitive to the degree of danger they faced. For example, before fishing in the safer inner waters of the lagoon,

Trobrianders employed relatively routine forms of magical rituals. But those who fished in the more dangerous open waters of the sea performed much more elaborate magic. Malinowski concluded that magic was found whenever there was fear and uncertainty.

A more recent example of the relationship between external stressors and superstition comes from research conducted during a different conflict. In the early weeks of the first Gulf War of 1990–1, Scud missiles were being launched from Iraq into Israel, and because there were fears that the Iraqis might use poisonous gas, many people established sealed rooms in their homes into which they fled in an attack. During this difficult period, many Israelis endorsed a number of superstitions related to their sealed rooms and other aspects of the bombings. Some people believed that it was bad luck to allow someone whose house had been hit by a missile into their sealed room. Others believed it was important to step into their sealed room right foot first. These magical beliefs were so common that television news commentators described how to use them. A clever researcher, Giora Keinan, realized that Tel Aviv was being hit by the Scuds but Jerusalem appeared to be out of range. Taking advantage of a unique research opportunity, Keinan went door to door interviewing people in both cities about their level of stress and the superstitions they used. He found that people who lived in Tel Aviv were more stressed and using more superstitions than people in Jerusalem. So, taken together, Malinowski and Keinan showed that superstition is more prevalent in situations where there are external uncertainties and dangers.

To the extent the residents of Tel Aviv and the Trobriand Islands were anxious, their circumstances produced what psychologists call *state anxiety*, a kind of anxiety that comes and goes depending upon what you are facing at the moment. In contrast, *trait anxiety* is assumed to be a more permanent feature of your personality, and people differ in their natural base level of anxiety. Trait anxiety has also been studied in relation to superstitious belief with the predictable finding that people who are more anxious are more likely to be superstitious.

Superstition and control. In almost every instance, superstition fills a gap. Often what is lacking is control. A football goalie, a person being interviewed for a job, and a stage actor all face circumstances that are both important and uncertain. If these people could be sure of always being successful, there would be no need for superstition, but goalies sometimes let the ball go through; job applicants often are not hired; and actors sometimes flub their lines in front of hundreds of people. The previously mentioned research on luck suggested that it provided a welcome sense of control for believers, and researchers who study the psychology of control have found several connections to superstition.

People differ on a dimension researchers call *locus of control*. Some of us typically feel that we are the masters of our own fates. Others feel tossed around by the winds of life. The first condition describes someone with internal locus of control (in charge), and the second is someone with external locus of control (not in charge). Several studies have found that, on average, people with external locus of control are more likely to be superstitious than internals. External locus of control makes superstition an attractive way to gain control. In contrast, people with internal locus of control have less need for superstition.

People also have different levels of desire for control in their lives, and, in another study, Keinan examined the combined effect of desire for control and stress on superstition. In a laboratory setting he interviewed college students using a set of questions that, in some cases, were designed to elicit knocking on wood (e.g. 'Has anyone in your immediate family suffered from lung cancer?'). Half of the participants were interviewed during a time of stress—just before an exam—and the others were interviewed on a normal, non-exam day. Keinan also gave each participant a desire for control scale and analysed the results separately for people who were high and low in desire for control. Keinan's knocking on wood questions worked, and he had two main findings: (1) as we would expect based on the Gulf War study, people under stress knocked more than those who were not and (2) people who were both stressed and high on desire for control knocked on wood the most. Keinan's studies suggest that being anxious or under stress creates a sense of loss of control, and that people employ superstition in an effort to regain control.

A bundle of negative traits. In addition to these personality dimensions, many studies have found that superstitiousness is correlated with a number of unpleasant traits, including depression, pessimism, neuroticism, and fear of death. However, if there is a ray of hope, it is that these correlations are real but very small. This means that personality dimensions can only go so far in helping us understand why someone is superstitious. Other factors, such as the nature of our upbringing and modes of thinking, are required to fill in the picture.

Learning superstitions

Many of the superstitions that people employ everyday are personal. They devise them on their own, and they generally do not advertise them to others. Typically, the superstition grows out of some coincidence. An athlete establishes a pre-game ritual that appears to be lucky, and so they keep using it on every game day. Before the ritual can be imbued with magical powers, the athlete may have to believe in luck as a force that can be summoned, but it is the coincidence of events that locks in the particular ritual. As mentioned in Chapter 4, the baseball player Wade Boggs believed that eating chicken before a game would improve his hitting. His superstition began when, as a high school student, he ate chicken before a baseball game and went on to get a hit all four times he batted. From that day forward, he continued to eat chicken before every game, a habit that he maintained throughout his seventeen-year-long professional career.

For over a century, psychologists have studied the way we solve problems and learn, and it may surprise you to know that they have spent considerable time investigating the way personal superstitions are acquired. One of the earliest and most famous studies of superstition was done with pigeons. American psychologist B. F. Skinner placed a hungry pigeon into a small chamber that—over his objections—eventually became known as a 'Skinner box'. Using an automatic food hopper on one side of the chamber, Skinner allowed the bird a couple of seconds' access to grain every fifteen seconds, regardless of what it was doing. Initially the bird was fairly passive, but it soon developed a stereotyped movement that it repeated over and over again. Different birds trained under these conditions developed different movements: one repeatedly pecked at a point on the floor, and another bobbed its head up and down. Skinner called his experiment '"Superstition" in the Pigeon', because the birds behaved as if they thought their chosen ritual caused the grain hopper to operate. Skinner's interpretation was that some random behaviour coincided with the appearance of food, and, as a result, it was repeated. It was a case of accidental or, as Skinner called it, 'adventitious' reinforcement. When he published this famous article, Skinner placed the word superstition in quotes because it was difficult to say what the pigeons believed. Superstition is a human concept that cannot be easily applied to pigeons.

Other researchers took issue with Skinner's original superstition experiment, arguing that the pigeons were showing forms of instinctive behaviour that emerge in the presence of food, but a number of investigators went on to conduct experiments with children and college students who produced very similar forms of superstition-like behaviour that was unlikely to be instinctive.

One of the most dramatic of examples was a study of Japanese college students conducted by Koichi Ono. He placed students in a booth and told them the object was to get as many points as

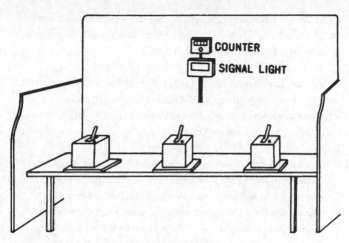

14. Drawing of the booth used in Ono's human superstition experiment.

possible to appear on an electronic counter in front of them. As shown in Figure 14, the booth included a table outfitted with three levers, and there was a signal light that could be illuminated red, green, or orange. Unknown to the participants, the levers were not connected to the point counter in any way, and although the signal light alternated among the three colours randomly, it also bore no relation to the way points were delivered. Similar to Skinner's pigeon study, Ono programmed the points to appear in a variable time schedule, regardless of what the students did.

As you can imagine, many participants pulled the levers in an effort to get the points to come, and, much like Skinner's pigeons, when a student did something just as a point was delivered, a pattern of behaviour was often stamped in. Most of the students developed unique combinations of lever pulls that were sustained for several minutes, and others had briefer periods of repeated patterns that faded away or were replaced by new ones.

In addition, a number of people pulled the levers much more rapidly when the signal light was a particular colour, despite the light being irrelevant to point delivery.

While they participated in the study, the students were observed through a one-way mirror in the wall of the room, and one of the students produced a truly remarkable sequence of superstitious behaviours, as reported by Ono:

> About 5 min into the session, a point delivery occurred after she had stopped pulling the lever temporarily and had put her right hand on the lever frame. This behavior was followed by a point delivery, after which she climbed on the table and put her right hand to the counter. Just as she did so, another point was delivered. Thereafter she began to touch many things in turn, such as the signal light, the screen, a nail on the screen, and the wall. About 10 min later, a point was delivered just as she jumped to the floor, and touching was replaced by jumping. After five jumps, a point was delivered when she jumped and touched the ceiling with her slipper in her hand. Jumping to touch the ceiling continued repeatedly and was followed by points until she stopped about 25 min into the session, perhaps because of fatigue.

Fatigue indeed! Humans are a remarkably intelligent species, and our ability to solve problems based on trial-and-error learning has been central to our success. But sometimes we arrive at a mistaken solution. We make connections between things that are unconnected. Because there is often little harm in these errors, they tend to persist, and, as we will see, there are some circumstances in which they might even help.

Superstitious thinking

So now that you've acquired a superstition—either because other people have taught you or because you have discovered some lucky ritual of your own—what sustains it? What kept Wade Boggs eating chicken for over seventeen years? Cognitive psychologists study how we reason and think, and in recent decades they have discovered a number of common biases and errors that plague our reasoning, some of which apply to the case of superstition. One is the well-known principle of *confirmation bias*. Once we have adopted an idea or belief as our own, it tends to colour our memory and actions. This is most obvious when people have strongly felt political values which bias their views of the news they hear. In addition, there is a natural tendency to search for information that bolsters your own viewpoint and forget or misremember information that contradicts your beliefs.

A related concept is *illusory correlation*. When we think about whether two things are connected, we often forget all of the relevant data we need to consider. The person who is superstitious tends to focus on the times the superstition is followed by success. They tend not to think about the times they were successful without the superstition or when the superstition failed. In the case of Wade Boggs's chicken eating, it was impossible to know whether it worked or not because he never tried to hit without eating chicken.

It should also be mentioned that Boggs was an excellent hitter. He won the American League batting title three times and was elected to the Baseball Hall of Fame. So, to some degree he can't be blamed for thinking that his superstition worked. Indeed, researchers have found that among school athletes, the better players employ the most superstitions. There are probably two reasons for this. Assuming that the better players are the stars of their teams, they have more to lose from a slump in performance, and, as we have seen, fear is a great motivation for superstition. The second-string bench players, on the other hand, probably have fewer worries. Second, if you are a better player, your superstitions appear to work. They may have nothing to do with your success, but as long as you employ your superstitions faithfully and keep performing well, there is no evidence to contradict your belief.

Illusions of control. Our desire for control is so strong that we see it where it isn't. There are so many times and places where we want to have control, but control is impossible. Of course, that does not stop us from trying and from sometimes believing that we do have control. In a classic experiment, college students were recruited for a study of psychokinesis. They were asked to concentrate on a die in an effort to psychically control how it would turn up, and each time the die was rolled, participants were asked how confident they were in their ability to influence the outcome. The experimenters arranged for students to toss the die into a funnel so that it landed in a box out of view, which ensured that the confidence ratings were not influenced by the outcome of the previous roll. In one version of the experiment there were two participants, one who was active—actually rolling the die into the funnel—and one who was merely looking on. Although the process of rolling dice is completely random and beyond anyone's influence, students who actually rolled the die were significantly more confident in their ability to influence the outcome.

In a separate study, the experimenters found that participants who were 'internals' on the trait of locus of control reported greater confidence in their ability to influence the die than those who were 'externals'. So, in combination, the findings on both locus of control and the illusion of control research suggest that superstition provides a sense of control when control is lacking. Merely taking some action—wearing a lucky piece of jewellery, crossing your fingers, or knocking on wood—provides a much-needed illusion of control. Whether the desired outcome happens or not, the psychological benefits of feeling more in control may be enough to sustain superstitious behaviour.

Fears of tempting fate. An interesting line of research looks at people's fears about tempting fate, or what is more commonly known as the jinx. Prospective students often buy T-shirts from colleges they hope to attend, but, according to legend, you risk being jinxed if you wear a college's shirt before hearing from the admissions office. In one study, participants read a story about a young man named Jon who was waiting to hear about his application to attend graduate school at Stanford University when his optimistic mother sent him a Stanford T-shirt. Half the participants read a version of the story that said Jon put the T-shirt away in a drawer and the other half were told that he wore the T-shirt the next day. When asked how likely Jon was to receive an acceptance letter from Stanford, the participants gave him a significantly lower chance if he wore the shirt. The jinx is real—at least in the minds of these participants.

Indeed, the jinx is real enough that some Israeli women are willing to spend considerable sums to avoid it. There is a common Jewish superstition that parents should wait to decorate a baby's room until after the child is born. Although no such offer is made for other kinds of furniture, several large department stores in Israel allow parents to pay for baby furniture well before the birth but have it delivered only after the baby arrives, and according to some reports, approximately 50 per cent of customers accept the delayed delivery option. In an experiment, pregnant Israeli women were asked to fill out a questionnaire about paranormal and superstitious beliefs—although not about this specific superstition—and were allowed to participate in a lottery to obtain either cash or baby furniture based on a coin flip. But before the lottery they were given the opportunity to report what they would choose if offered either a gift certificate for baby furniture worth 3,000 NIS (approximately 860 US dollars) or several different cash amounts, varying between 3,000 and 0 NIS. There was a catch, however. For half of the participants, if they won the gift certificate for baby furniture, the furniture had to be delivered immediately. For the other half of the women, the delivery date was flexible and could be up to a year later. The results were that, when delivery had to be immediate, women who endorsed popular superstitions were willing to accept substantially lower sums of money in lieu of the furniture than those who had the option of delaying delivery. This effect was stronger for women who were in the second half of their pregnancy.

These superstitious jinxes are thought to be sustained by our imaginings of the various outcomes. It is one thing to be rejected from a college or to have problems with a pregnancy, but it is quite another to have these unfortunate events happen when you have acted with hubris (in the T-shirt case) or violated a social norm (in the baby furniture example). Negative outcomes under these circumstances would add insult to injury, and, as a result, decisions about whether to wear the college T-shirt or accept the baby furniture immediately are motivated by fear of these doubly negative outcomes. Furthermore, the imagined catastrophe is so salient that, at least in the college T-shirt experiment, onlookers believe it is more likely to happen if the student tempts fate.

Do superstitions help or harm?

Now that we have followed superstitions through millennia and have uncovered some of the psychological forces that keep them alive, we might pause and ask the simple question, 'Are superstitions good for us?' I will save the larger social and cultural implications of this question for Chapter 6, but what about individual people who hold on to superstitious beliefs and behaviours? The very fact that superstition has such a long history suggests we must get something out of it.

Before going further, we should deal with one question right away: there is no magic. There is no evidence that superstitions have a direct cause-and-effect relationship on anything in the natural world. Neither astrology, nor homeopathy, nor palm reading, nor eating chicken before batting have sufficient empirical evidence to suggest they work. Nor is there evidence that Friday the 13th or black cats are unlucky. So, if superstitions have good or bad effects, we must look elsewhere.

As we have seen in this chapter, there are many paths to acquiring and maintaining superstitious beliefs and behaviour, and, as a result, anyone who has the right background or temperament will be inclined to employ a superstition when the circumstances warrant it. But judging the value of the behaviour is another thing. We all do things that fall on different sides of the beneficial/non-beneficial line. We have bad habits and good. What about superstition?

In the commercial world, research shows that products that are associated with a lucky superstition are evaluated more positively than ones that are not, but from the consumer's point of view, this could be either a good thing or a bad thing, depending upon the individual's economic circumstances. A more clearly negative effect of superstition can be seen in the relationship between gambling behaviour and belief in luck. One of the strongest predictors of problem gambling is impulsivity, but belief in good luck is also higher among problem gamblers than among non-problem gamblers. In addition, problem gamblers have a stronger illusion of control. In comparison to non-problem gamblers, they believe they have a greater power over the outcome of their bets. So, superstitious ideas about luck and control may encourage self-defeating gambling behaviour, and, based on a coldly statistical analysis, we might reason that, if these beliefs prolong your stay at the roulette table, most of the time you will go home with less money.

The illusion of control can often be seen as a kind of mistaken view of the situation at hand. If you are at the casino playing dice, the outcome of the roll is completely random. Some players believe that by tossing the dice in a particular way they can control the result. Typically, players use a gentle roll for a low number and a harder toss for a high number. All of these actions suggest players see dice-rolling as a skilled activity over which they have some control. This is decidedly not the case. Tossing dice is an ancient random number generator whose origins go back to early divination methods, such as the casting of lots or tossing of yarrow sticks. Similarly, the spins of the roulette wheel and the slot machine are random events over which we have no control. But these random processes are often approached as if they were skilled activities.

However, superstitions are not limited to random processes. They are also commonly employed during job interviews, theatrical performances, and sports contests, all of which require genuine skill. So, even if there is no actual magic involved, can employing a superstition have tangible benefits in a skilled activity? Here our chances are better because the effect would presumably be psychological. We know that superstition arises during periods of stress and anxiety. If employing a superstition helps tamp down our anxieties, it might improve performance.

Perhaps somewhat surprisingly, so far there is not much evidence to support this hypothesis. Things appeared hopeful when, in 2010, a group of researchers at the University of Cologne published a very simple study of people putting a golf ball into a cup in a laboratory. Half of the participants were handed a golf ball and told, 'This is your ball', and the other half were told, 'This ball has been lucky today'. Previously, the researchers had determined that approximately 80 per cent of the people in the subject pool believed in luck. Miraculously, when asked to putt the ball into the cup, the lucky ball group had significantly more successes than the other group. In a number of other experiments, the Cologne group seemed to demonstrate that superstitions could bolster self-confidence and improve performance at a skilled activity. As odd as it might seem, no one had previously published such a clear example of the positive effects of superstition, and the golf ball study created quite a splash—until someone tried to replicate it. In 2014 a group of researchers at the Dominican University in the USA designed a much larger and more rigorous version of the golf ball study, but in this case the lucky ball group did no better than the control group.

One might attribute the different results to cultural differences between the German participants in the original study and Americans in the replication, but the Dominican researchers were careful to duplicate the levels of belief in luck reported in the original study. As a result, we are left with a murky story. It still seems plausible that employing a superstition could boost confidence and, in turn, performance of a skill. Unfortunately, as of this writing, we have no solid evidence to back up this hypothesis. But all is not lost.

Many superstitions emerge when there is time to fill. Actors and athletes often have to wait before they go on stage or take the field, and establishing a ritual can help to focus the mind in a mantra-like way. Robert Plant, lead singer of the legendary British rock band Led Zeppelin, was said to sip a cup of tea while ironing his own shirts prior to performances, a ritual he said got him 'in the mood'. Many athletes and performers refer to these rituals as 'routines' and downplay any magical significance, but it is clear that others treat their rituals as a kind of incantation.

In 2016 Alison Wood Brooks and colleagues published a study of the psychological effects of rituals. First, they conducted an online survey to determine how common it was for people to employ a ritual prior to an important event such as an athletic performance or a job interview. Forty-six per cent of participants said they used some kind of ritual in these circumstances, and 20 per cent of those who used a ritual said it had superstitious elements, such as knocking on wood or crossing fingers. They then went on to conduct a number of experiments in which, upon arriving at the laboratory, participants learned that they would be doing something rather stressful, such as singing the song 'Don't Stop Believin'' by the rock group Journey in front of an experimenter or completing some anxiety-provoking maths problems. Some participants were asked to complete a ritual prior to singing or solving problems:

> Please count out loud slowly up to 10 from 0, then count back down to 0. You should say each number out loud and write each number on the piece of paper in front of you as you say it. You may use the entire paper. Sprinkle salt on your paper. Crinkle up your paper. Throw your paper in the trash.

In each case, when participants performed a ritual prior to singing or solving, they reported lower levels of anxiety and did better. Singers made fewer errors as measured by a karaoke machine and problem solvers got more answers correct. Brooks's research showed clear evidence that rituals lowered anxiety, which in turn improved performance. Interestingly, the same sequence of activities, when described as 'random behaviours', did not improve anxiety and performance, but, when described as 'a ritual', they did. So, at least for superstitious rituals, we have evidence that they can improve performance in a skilled activity. But the research suggests that it is the ritual—not the superstition—that does the work. Nonetheless, if a superstitious ritual works, it is likely to be repeated.

It makes sense that superstitions might have psychological benefits that have kept them going over the ages. So far, the actual empirical evidence in support of this view is not particularly strong, but Brooks's study of superstition provides some encouragement, at least with respect to rituals. Studies of paranormal beliefs—some of which overlap with superstition—show opposing effects of belief on happiness and income. For example, a large-scale survey of Japanese adults found that people with higher levels of paranormal belief reported higher levels of happiness compared to people with lower levels of paranormal belief. This finding is consistent with other studies showing that religious people are happier than non-religious people. However, the Japanese study also showed that paranormal believers had significantly lower incomes.

In the case of astrology, a relatively elaborate system of belief, there is some evidence that people use it as a coping mechanism. Finnish researchers Outi Lillqvist and Marjaana Lindeman conducted a study of people attending adult education classes in either introduction to astrology, psychology, or German language. They found that, when compared to psychology and German students, the astrology students had recently experienced significantly more life crises. In addition, even among the psychology and German comparison groups, people with greater belief in astrology also reported more life crises. If these people were using astrology as a stabilizing force in their lives, it would be consistent with reports that millennials in the USA are both less religious than previous generations and more attracted to astrology.

We don't have any evidence of the effectiveness of astrology for providing spiritual solace or comfort in times of trouble, and the Japanese study did not allow for conclusions about cause and effect, but these studies suggest that, when used as general coping mechanisms, paranormal and superstitious beliefs provide—at best—a mixture of costs and benefits. In the case of some specific superstitions, there are more definite drawbacks. For example, I see no value in the fear-based superstitions. They may have once satisfied the need to explain why bad things happen, but I am of the opinion that today we would be much better off if no one had bothered to teach us about black cats, the number thirteen, or the evil eye. Once you learn about these foreboding signs, you are faced with an unwanted dilemma whenever they appear. Speaking only for myself, this is not something I would choose.

Some superstitions have the potential for much more substantial harms. As we have seen, belief in luck is more common among problem gamblers, and other forms of superstition can also be quite costly. Telephone and internet psychics charge by the minute for their services, and, as a result, their clients can rack up substantial bills talking to someone who claims to have abilities they don't actually have. Finally, those who choose homeopathy or other unscientific medical treatments over conventional science-based medicine often do so at substantial risk. In 2012 a 19-month-old boy died of meningitis when his parents treated him for two weeks with naturopathic medicines and only took him to the doctor after he stopped breathing. Some superstitious actions are genuinely harmful, but, evaluated on a simple utilitarian basis, the great majority of common superstitions are relatively inexpensive and harmless. Furthermore, although the evidence is not strong, they may help reduce anxiety and provide a welcome illusion of control.

Chapter 6
The future of superstition

The study of superstition

People have been fascinated with superstition for a very long time, and that fascination is unlikely to end soon. Books and articles on the history of superstition, magic, witchcraft, and spiritualism continue to be written, and there is much more to learn about superstition's past. Indeed, superstition's past isn't even past. The Enlightenment may be over 200 years behind us, but demonology is alive and well. For the first time, in May 2019, the Vatican opened its course on how to perform exorcisms to members of other faiths. People still believe in the devil, and exorcists still use consecrated objects and prayer in their battles with demons. The long history of superstition is still unfolding.

In recent years, a growing group of psychologists and sociologists have been studying superstition. Questionnaires to measure superstitious belief have been translated into several languages, and a recent magnetic resonance imaging (MRI) study revealed that a small area of the right frontal lobe was more active when participants made decisions based on good luck. But perhaps the most popular area of research today is the role of superstition in consumer choice. This effort has probably been encouraged by the rapid growth of the Chinese consumer market, and, as a result, this line of investigation is likely to continue.

We have already seen that in the Chinese market red products are evaluated more positively and advertised prices tend to favour the number eight and avoid the number four. The influence of unlucky hotel floor and room numbers has also been a subject of research. Previous studies have shown the effects of feng shui on prices in the residential real estate market, but feng shui is also widely considered in the design of corporate buildings in Asia in an effort to manage corporate image. Buildings that violate the principles of feng shui can bring negative attention. For example, the Bank of China Tower in Hong Kong, designed by I. M. Pei, was criticized by feng shui experts for its 'troublesome' use of triangles on the glass façade. All of which suggests that feng shui is likely to be a topic of future research.

But not all studies of consumer superstition are based in the Asian market. For example, researchers have sought to employ a variety of superstitions to promote customer loyalty at casinos, and in 2016, Bally Gaming, Inc. patented a slot machine design that would provide various forms of feedback in response to players' superstitious screen gestures, such as tapping the screen while the wheels are spinning. A recent sports marketing study found that US fans who engaged in team-related superstitions had more positive feelings about the game—even when the team lost.

Much of the audience for this research is likely to be various business and marketing interests. For example, a recent study of hotel guests in Hong Kong showed that Chinese guests were more bothered by unlucky floor or room numbers than western guests, and the authors made this specific recommendation:

> All else being equal, we suggest that hotels assign a luck-enhancing floor and room number ('8' or those ending with '8') to younger, independently travelling, and business Chinese tourists, particularly when they appear in distress or subpar mood (e.g. a delayed flight).

Similarly, the authors of the US sports marketing study mentioned above suggested that sports organizations could build greater fan engagement by encouraging fan superstitions. The profit motive is a powerful force, but there are a number of ethical questions that attend to these studies. Whether it is their intention or not, social scientists who conduct consumer research on superstition are likely to encourage the role of irrational behaviour in the marketplace and beyond. In a free market system there are few limits on the sale of bogus products and services. Psychics and fortune tellers openly advertise talents they do not possess, and Amazon.com and Etsy.com offer page after page of spell kits, lucky horseshoes, and four-leaf clovers. In the USA homeopathic medicines are sold over the counter at drug stores without any labelling to indicate that they contain no active ingredients at all. When there is money to be made, it is unlikely that those who stand to gain will be inhibited by the prospect of promoting irrational behaviour, and, with few exceptions, governments have been reluctant to regulate these markets. Reason falls away when unreason pays. Which brings us to the question of superstition's larger cultural role.

Superstition and society

The most likely thing that can be said about the future of superstition is that it will always be with us. The same psychological forces that motivated Theophrastus' Superstitious Man to wash himself in three different springs before starting his day still motivate modern bingo players who cling to lucky figurines and hopeful lovers who consult their horoscopes. Although human civilization has eliminated many of the uncertainties faced by ancient peoples, countless important life events are still beyond our control, and when there is uncertainty, magic finds a welcome home. Nonetheless, we might ask, what manner of superstition lies ahead?

We are often in two minds about superstition. When asked about why he was going to copy and forward a chain letter, Gene

Foreman, an editor at *The Philadelphia Inquirer*, said, 'You understand that I am not doing this because I'm superstitious, I just want to avoid bad luck.' This is a very common experience. People often recognize that superstitions are silly and irrational, but they are still moved to employ them. 'I don't want to take a chance.' We experience a similar kind of internal conflict when we are tempted by the strawberry cheesecake dessert, while knowing it would be better to pass it by. In the case of superstition, American psychologist Jane Risen has suggested a theory based on the idea that we have two mental processing systems, a quick-acting intuitive system and a more deliberative rational system. According to Risen, when thinking about a superstition, our intuitive mind often wants to go along with it, but our rational side wants to correct our intuitions and move us to reject magical thinking. However, people often acquiesce to their intuitive brain and, following Foreman's lead, give in to superstition. When we know it's Friday the 13th, we may decide it's not a good day to trade on the stock market, despite understanding there is nothing to back up the superstition.

Building upon Risen's theory, we might anticipate three kinds of reactions to superstition: one that involves this I-am-of-two-minds kind of conflict and two that do not. First, there are people for whom superstition is not a real option. They are rationalists whose background was relatively free of socialization into the world of superstition, and, for them, genuine superstitious intuitions never arrive. On the opposite end of the spectrum are the true believers, for whom there is also little conflict. They may be aware of social taboos against advertising your superstitions, but these believers are otherwise not in conflict because their deliberative rational side never engages. They take precautions against the evil eye and don't give it a second thought. Finally, there are Risen's acquiescers who fall somewhere between the other two groups. Despite a rational understanding that there is no magic in the world, they give in to intuition and don't

114

travel or schedule doctor's appointments on the thirteenth day of the month.

From a societal point of view, we have little to worry about from either the determined rationalists or the acquiescers. Both are grounded in reason, and if sometimes they give in to superstitious intuitions, they do so without relinquishing reason altogether. No, if there is anyone we have to worry about, it is the true believers. As we have seen, there are some superstitions that are potentially costly and dangerous, but true believers pose a different threat that is less about their superstitions and more about the thinking that supports them.

As we have seen, superstition is a transactional concept. It has no inherent meaning of its own. It is a term that only gains meaning in relation to some different, more accepted world-view. Today that more accepted view is most often the accumulated knowledge of science, but, as we have seen, fashions change. *Homo sapiens* took many millennia to stumble upon the system of logic and evidence we now associate with science, and there is no guarantee it will remain dominant. In a book called *Enlightenment Now*, psychologist Steven Pinker argued that in recent centuries, the quality of life has substantially improved—not just in the usual places but across the globe. Poverty and death from war and disease have all diminished, and life expectancy, economic security, and happiness have grown. Furthermore, Pinker argues that these changes can be attributed to the Enlightenment values of reason, science, and humanism. Even if we grant Pinker's conclusion, it is prudent to ask, is continued progress inevitable? Modern democracy, one of the great embodiments of Enlightenment thinking, is barely 300 years old. Before it emerged, sheer concentrated power ruled the world. As I write this, Europe and the United States have seen a rise in authoritarianism and anti-democratic values, and, despite the broad appeal of Enlightenment ideas, religious dogmatism still

controls large swathes of the globe. It is not a given that
democracy will continue to spread.

Much of the shared knowledge that created the improvements of
modern life appears to be under threat, and there is evidence that
experts have become devalued—including scientists. For example,
there is overwhelming medical consensus that vaccines have
played a major role in the eradication of many diseases and
substantially lengthened average life expectancies. The list of
forgotten plagues includes measles, diphtheria, chicken pox,
rubella, polio, and whooping cough, among many others.
Yet unfounded fears about a presumed link between childhood
vaccination and autism have led to diminished trust in vaccines
and reduced rates of inoculation in many affluent nations.
A 2018 poll of European Union countries found that vaccination
rates had declined in twelve EU member states and that in
Sweden only 56.5 per cent of adults surveyed believed that the
measles-mumps-rubella (MMR) vaccine was safe. Measles, which
was declared eliminated in the USA in 2000, has come back.
By April of 2019, a record 695 cases were recorded, with large
outbreaks among Orthodox Jewish communities in New York
and Michigan that had low rates of vaccination. In 2012, the USA
saw 48,277 cases of whooping cough, the highest rate since 1955.

Climate change, arguably one of the most pressing problems of
modern times, has emerged as a largely political rather than
scientific issue in the USA. Again, there is overwhelming scientific
consensus that global warming is real and at least partly due to
human activity, yet belief varies dramatically with political
affiliation. A 2018 Gallup poll found that the statement 'Global
warming is caused by human activities' was endorsed by 89 per cent
of Democrats but only 35 per cent of Republicans.

It is ironic that one of the most dazzling symbols of science in our
everyday lives—the Internet—has helped to promulgate false
information and cloud the difference between truth and bunk.

Most of the time, superstition is just fine. It causes little harm, and it may provide a welcome psychological benefit. As someone who endorses the value of science and reason, I would not encourage anyone who has not already done so to adopt a superstition. But if there is superstition in our future, I suspect its real value will be as a bellwether of other problems.

Some may suggest that science is just another system of belief that is not fundamentally different from the religious systems that banished superstition and magic into the past. This argument misses the point. Science is most properly understood as a collection of methods for finding the truth. As Carl Sagan once said, 'The method of science is tried and true. It is not perfect, it is just the best we have. And to abandon it, with its skeptical protocols, is the pathway to a dark age.' Unlike organized religion, science is not dogmatic. New knowledge often overthrows old ideas that are proved wrong. Furthermore, the natural world, as revealed by science, continues on its ancient path, whether you believe in it or not. But if sufficient numbers of people abandon scientific thinking and dismiss the accumulated knowledge of scientists, we risk losing the benefits of the Enlightenment. If we move in that direction, rising levels of superstition will be a symptom of a more fundamental problem. We may cling to many of the technological fruits of science, but if we abandon reason and evidence in our effort to solve social problems, we risk falling back into the brutal worlds of the past.

References

Chapter 1: The origins of superstition

I Ching divination and Chun hexagram: Hellmut Wilhelm (ed.), *The I Ching or Book of Changes* (Princeton University Press, 1997), 16–20.

Ancient Egyptian magic: Geraldine Pinch, *Magic in Ancient Egypt*, revised edition (University of Texas Press, 2010).

Pythagoras' magical powers: Daniel Ogden, *Magic, Witchcraft, and Ghosts in the Greek and Roman Worlds: A Sourcebook*, 2nd edition (Oxford University Press, USA, 2009), 9–13.

Ancient Egyptian medicine: Geraldine Pinch, *Magic in Ancient Egypt*, revised edition (University of Texas Press, 2010), 133–6.

Binding curses: Christopher A. Faraone, 'The Agonistic Context of Early Greek Binding Spells', in Christopher A. Faraone and Dirk Obbink (eds), *Magika Hiera: Ancient Greek Magic and Religion*, 3–32. (Oxford University Press, 1991).

Translation of Bath curse tablet: D. R. Jordan, 'Curses from the Waters of Sulis', *Journal of Roman Archeology* 3 (1990): 437–41.

On *deisidaimonia* and *superstitio*: Richard Gordon, 'Superstitio, Superstition and Religious Repression in the Late Roman Republic and Principate (100BCE–300CE)', *Past and Present* 72 (suppl. 3) (2008): 72–94.

Theophrastus quote: Hugh Bowden, 'Before Superstition and After: Theophrastus and Plutarch on Deisidaimonia', *Past and Present* 199 (suppl. 3) (2008): 57.

Plutarch on the atheist and superstitious man: Plutarch, 'On Superstition' (*De superstitione*) (Loeb Classical Library, 1928). <http://penelope.uchicago.edu/Thayer/E/Roman/Texts/Plutarch/Moralia/De_superstitione*.html>.

Cicero on *superstitio*: S. A. Smith, 'Introduction', *Past and Present* 199
(suppl. 3) (2008): 7–55; Marcus Tullius Cicero, trans. H. Rackham,
De natura deorum; Academica (Harvard University Press, 1933), 113.

Chapter 2: Religious superstition

Judaism and pagan rituals: Michael David Bailey, *Magic and
Superstition in Europe: A Concise History from Antiquity to the
Present* (Rowman & Littlefield, 2007), 41.

Celsus on Jesus as magician: Dale B. Martin, *Inventing Superstition:
From Hippocratics to the Christians* (Harvard University Press,
2004), 144–5.

Pliny the Younger 'depraved immoderate *superstitio*' and Tacitus on
Nero and the Christians: Dale B. Martin, *Inventing Superstition:
From Hippocratics to the Christians* (Harvard University Press,
2004), 2–4.

Celsus v. Origen: Stephen Benko, *Pagan Rome and the Early
Christians* (Indiana University Press, 1984), 117–19;
Dale B. Martin, *Inventing Superstition: From Hippocratics to the
Christians* (Harvard University Press, 2004), 140–86.

Firmicus v. Firmicus: Michele R. Salzman, '"Superstitio" in the "Codex
Theodosianus" and the Persecution of Pagans', *Vigiliae Christianae*
41(2) (1987): 172–88.

Augustine: Asher Ovadiah and Sonia Mucznik, 'Deisidaimonia,
Superstitio and Religio: Graeco-Roman, Jewish and Early
Christian Concepts', *Liber Annuus* 64 (2014): 417–40.

The *indiculus superstitionum*: S. A. Smith, 'Introduction', *Past and
Present* 199 (suppl. 3) (2008): 7–55.

Weather magic: Michael David Bailey, *Magic and Superstition in
Europe: A Concise History from Antiquity to the Present* (Rowman
& Littlefield, 2007), 69–70.

Lothar II and Theutberga: Stuart Airlie, 'Private Bodies and the Body
Politic in the Divorce Case of Lothar II', *Past and Present* 161
(1998): 3–38.

Famine and plague: Ole Jørgen Benedictow, *The Black Death,
1346–53: The Complete History* (Boydell & Brewer, 2004); Ian
Kershaw, 'The Great Famine and Agrarian Crisis in England
1315–1322', *Past and Present* 59 (May 1973): 3–50.

Hansel and Gretel: Neil Gaiman, *Hansel and Gretel* (Toon Books,
2014), 52–3.

Gratian and inquisitors: Michael D. Bailey, 'Concern over Superstition in Late Medieval Europe', *The Religion of Fools? Superstition Past and Present* 199 (suppl. 3) (2008): 115–33.

Knights Templar and Bophomet: Michael David Bailey, *Magic and Superstition in Europe: A Concise History from Antiquity to the Present* (Rowman & Littlefield, 2007), 121.

Knights Templar and Friday the 13th: Nathaniel Lachenmeyer, *13: The Story of the World's Most Popular Superstition* (Running Press, 2004).

Witchcraft and witch trials: Michael David Bailey, *Magic and Superstition in Europe: A Concise History from Antiquity to the Present* (Rowman & Littlefield, 2007), 119–40.

Chapter 3: The secularization of superstition

Ficino and hermetic magic: Frances A. Yates, 'The Hermetic Tradition in the Renaissance', in Charles Singleton (ed.), *Art, Science, and History in the Renaissance*, 255–74 (The Johns Hopkins Press, 1968).

Pico della Mirandola: Michael David Bailey, *Magic and Superstition in Europe: A Concise History from Antiquity to the Present* (Rowman & Littlefield, 2007), 186–8; Frank L. Borchardt, 'The Magus as Renaissance Man', *Sixteenth Century Journal* 21(1) (1990): 57–76.

Agrippa: George H. Daniels, Jr, 'Knowledge and Faith in the Thought of Cornelius Agrippa', *Bibliothèque d'Humanisme et Renaissance* 26(2) (1964): 326–40.

Edith Stein: Alessandra Stanley, 'A Jew's Odyssey from Catholic Nun to Saint', *The New York Times*, 11 October 1998.

Saints Christopher and Joseph, holy water, and communion host: Michael David Bailey, *Magic and Superstition in Europe: A Concise History from Antiquity to the Present* (Rowman & Littlefield, 2007); Keith Thomas, *Religion and the Decline of Magic: Studies in Popular Beliefs in Sixteenth and Seventeenth-Century England* (Penguin UK, 2003).

Consecrated wax: Euan Cameron, *Enchanted Europe: Superstition, Reason, and Religion 1250–1750* (Oxford University Press, 2010), 57.

Hunting for treasure: Keith Thomas, *Religion and the Decline of Magic: Studies in Popular Beliefs in Sixteenth and Seventeenth-Century England* (Penguin UK, 2003), 279–82.

Love charms and fortune telling: Michael D. Bailey, *Fearful Spirits,*
Reasoned Follies: The Boundaries of Superstition in Late Medieval
Europe (Cornell University Press, 2013); Keith Thomas, *Religion*
and the Decline of Magic: Studies in Popular Beliefs in Sixteenth
and Seventeenth-Century England (Penguin UK, 2003), 282–4.

Protestant views of Catholic ritual: Euan Cameron, *Enchanted*
Europe: Superstition, Reason, and Religion 1250–1750 (Oxford
University Press, 2010), 196–208; Helen Parish, '"Lying Histories
Fayning False Miracles": Magic, Miracles and Mediaeval History in
Reformation Polemic', *Reformation & Renaissance Review* 4(2)
(2002): 230–40; Keith Thomas, *Religion and the Decline of Magic:*
Studies in Popular Beliefs in Sixteenth and Seventeenth-Century
England (Penguin UK, 2003), 58–67.

European Wars of Religion and Spanish Inquisition: Robert Jean
Knecht, *The French Religious Wars 1562–1598* (Bloomsbury
Publishing, 2014); Cathal J. Nolan, *The Age of Wars of Religion,*
1000–1650: An Encyclopedia of Global Warfare and Civilization
(Greenwood Publishing Group, 2006).

Kramer, Sprenger, the *Malleus Maleficarum*, and Molitor: Michael
David Bailey, *Magic and Superstition in Europe: A Concise History*
from Antiquity to the Present (Rowman & Littlefield, 2007),
136–40.

Witch trial death estimates: Anne Llewellyn Barstow, *Witchcraze: A*
New History of the European Witch Hunts (Pandora, 1994), 22–3.

Explanation for witch trial phenomenon: Peter T. Leeson and
Jacob W. Russ, 'Witch Trials', *The Economic Journal* 128 (613)
(2017): 2066–105.

Castellio, Servetus, and Calvin and quotation from *Contra Libellum*
Calvini: Bruce Gordon, 'To Kill a Heretic: Sebastian Castellio
against John Calvin', in Geoff Kemp (ed.), *Censorship Moments:*
Reading Texts in the History of Censorship and Freedom of
Expression, 55–62 (Bloomsbury, 2015).

Scientific revolution: Keith Thomas, *Religion and the Decline of Magic:*
Studies in Popular Beliefs in Sixteenth and Seventeenth-Century
England (Penguin UK, 2003), 769–74.

Anna Göldi: Imogen Foulkes, 'Europe's Last Witch-hunt', BBC News,
20 September 2007 <http://news.bbc.co.uk/2/hi/programmes/
from_our_own_correspondent/7003128.stm>.

Challenging disenchantment: Richard Jenkins, 'Disenchantment,
Enchantment and Re-Enchantment: Max Weber at the
Millennium', *Max Weber Studies* 1 (2000): 11–32.

Chapter 4: Superstition in the modern world

Fox sisters: Ann Braude, *Radical Spirits: Spiritualism and Women's Rights in Nineteenth-Century America* (Indiana University Press, 2001), 10–25; Krister Dylan Knapp, *William James: Psychical Research and the Challenge of Modernity* (UNC Press Books, 2017), 26–38.

Banner of Light spiritual newspaper: Ann Braude, *Radical Spirits: Spiritualism and Women's Rights in Nineteenth-Century America* (Indiana University Press, 2001), 25–9; Arthur Conan Doyle, *The History of Spiritualism*, vol. 1 (The Psychic Bookshop, 1926).

Spiritualism and necromancy: A. B. Morrison, *Spiritualism and Necromancy* (Hitchcock and Walden, 1873).

Swedenborg: Arthur Conan Doyle, *The History of Spiritualism*, vol. 1 (The Psychic Bookshop, 1926).

Franz Mesmer: Douglas J. Lanska and Joseph T. Lanska, 'Franz Anton Mesmer and the Rise and Fall of Animal Magnetism: Dramatic Cures, Controversy, and Ultimately a Triumph for the Scientific Method', in Harry Whitaker, Christopher Upham Murray Smith, and Stanley Finger (eds), *Brain, Mind and Medicine: Essays in Eighteenth-Century Neuroscience*, 301–20 (New York: Springer, 2007); Régine Plas, 'Psychology and Psychical Research in France around the End of the 19th Century', *History of the Human Sciences* 25(2) (2012): 91–107.

William James's psychical research: Krister Dylan Knapp, *William James: Psychical Research and the Challenge of Modernity* (UNC Press Books, 2017).

William Mumler and psychic photography: Clément Chéroux, Pierre Apraxine, Andreas Fischer, Denis Canguilhem, and Sophie Schmit, *The Perfect Medium: Photography and the Occult* (Yale University Press, 2005), 20–8.

Superstition versus religion: Euan Cameron, *Enchanted Europe: Superstition, Reason, and Religion 1250–1750* (Oxford University Press, 2010), 303–10 (Voltaire quote from p. 306). David Hume, *Essays, Moral and Political* (printed by R. Fleming and A. Alison for A. Kincaid, 1741–2), vol. 1, 141–51.

Superstition versus mental illness: Peter Brugger and Isabelle Viaud-Delmon, *Dialogues in Clinical Neuroscience* 12(2) (2010): 250–3.

Definition of superstition: Gustav Jahoda, *The Psychology of Superstition* (Jason Aronson, 1974); Stuart Vyse, *Believing in*

Magic: The Psychology of Superstition (updated edition) (Oxford University Press, 2014), 22–7.

Superstitions in Utah: Anthon Steffensen Cannon, Wayland Debs Hand, and Jeannine Talley (eds), *Popular Beliefs and Superstitions from Utah* (University of Utah Press, 1984).

The number thirteen: Nathaniel Lachenmeyer, *13: The Story of the World's Most Popular Superstition* (Thunder's Mouth Press, 2004).

Evil eye: Allan S. Berger, 'The Evil Eye—An Ancient Superstition', *Journal of Religion and Health* 51(4) (2012): 1098–103; Pliny the Elder quote: Pliny the Elder, *The Natural History*, ed. John Bostock and H. T. Riley, VII, 2. <http://www.perseus.tufts.edu/hopper/text?doc=Perseus:text:1999.02.0137:book=7:chapter=2>.

Astrology: Nicholas Campion, Outi Lillqvist, and Marjaana Lindeman, 'Belief in Astrology as a Strategy for Self-Verification and Coping with Negative Life-Events', *European Psychologist* 3(3) (2004): 202–8; Alyssa Jayne Wyman and Stuart Vyse, 'Science versus the Stars: A Double-Blind Test of the Validity of the NEO Five-Factor Inventory and Computer-Generated Astrological Natal Charts', *Journal of General Psychology* 135(3) (2008): 287–300.

Homeopathy: E. Ernst, 'A Systematic Review of Systematic Reviews of Homeopathy', *British Journal of Clinical Pharmacology* 54 (2002): 577–82; David M. Shaw, 'Homeopathy Is Where the Harm Is: Five Unethical Effects of Funding Unscientific "Remedies"', *Journal of Medical Ethics* 36(3) (2010): 130–1.

Feng shui and *Qi*: Steven C. Bourassa and Vincent S. Peng, 'Hedonic Prices and House Numbers: The Influence of Feng Shui', *International Real Estate Review* 2(1) (1999): 79–93; Eric W. K. Tsang, 'Superstition and Decision-Making: Contradiction or Complement?' *Academy of Management Executive* 18(4) (2011): 92–104.

Chapter 5: The psychology of superstition

OnePoll.com Friday the 13th survey: 'Casumo—Bad Luck Holiday'. Drench Design. Accessed <https://www.drench-design.com/project/casumo-bad-luck-holiday/>.

IpsosMORI survey of beliefs: 'Survey on Beliefs'. Ipsos MORI. <https://www.ipsos.com/ipsos-mori/en-uk/survey-beliefs>.

Harris poll of US superstitious belief: 'Avoid Black Cats? Walk Around Ladders? Are Americans Superstitious?' The Harris Poll, 27 February 2014. <https://theharrispoll.com/

new-york-n-y-february-27-2014-do-you-walk-around-a-black-cat-or-always-throw-spilled-salt-over-your-shoulder-just-how-common-are-beliefs-in-certain-superstitions-many-americans-grew-up-hearin/>.

Gallup poll of attitudes toward rooms on the thirteenth floor: Joseph Carroll, 'Thirteen Percent of Americans Bothered to Stay on Hotels' 13th Floor'. Gallup.com, 15 March 2007. <https://news.gallup.com/poll/26887/thirteen-percent-americans-bothered-stay-hotels-13th-floor.aspx>.

Positive and negative superstitions: Richard Wiseman and Caroline Watt, 'Measuring Superstitious Belief: Why Lucky Charms Matter', *Personality and Individual Differences* 37(8) (2004): 1533–41.

Belief in luck: Peter R. Darke and Jonathan L. Freedman, 'The Belief in Good Luck Scale', *Journal of Research in Personality* 31(31) (1997): 486–511.

Superstition and personality: Stuart Vyse, *Believing in Magic: The Psychology of Superstition* (updated edition) (Oxford University Press, 2014).

Keinan studies of stress and superstitious belief: Giora Keinan, 'Effects of Stress and Tolerance of Ambiguity on Magical Thinking', *Journal of Personality and Social Psychology* 67(1) (1994): 48–55; Giora Keinan, 'The Effects of Stress and Desire for Control on Superstitious Behavior', *Personality and Social Psychology Bulletin* 28(1) (2002): 102–8.

B. F. Skinner's superstition experiment: B. F. Skinner, '"Superstition" in the Pigeon', *Journal of Experimental Psychology* 38(2) (1948): 168–272.

Ono's superstition experiment with college students: Koichi Ono, 'Superstitious Behavior in Humans', *Journal of the Experimental Analysis of Behavior* 47(3) (1987): 261–71. The description of the jumping participant is from p. 265.

Illusion of control: Oren Griffiths, Noor Shehabi, Robin A. Murphy, and Mike E. Le Pelley, 'Superstition Predicts Perception of Illusory Control', *British Journal of Psychology* 110(3) (2018): 499–518.

Die rolling and illusion of control: Victor A. Benassi, Paul D. Sweeney, and Gregg E. Drevno, 'Mind over Matter: Perceived Success at Psychokinesis Victor', *Journal of Personality and Social Psychology* 37(8) (1979): 1377–86.

The jinx and tempting fate: Ya'akov Bayer, Bradley J. Ruffle, Ze'ev Shtudiner, and Ro'i Zultan, 'Costly Superstitious Beliefs: Experimental Evidence' (2018) SSRN: <https://ssrn.com/

abstract=3148047 or http://dx.doi.org/10.2139/ssrn.3148047>
Jane L. Risen and Thomas Gilovich, 'Why People Are Reluctant to
Tempt Fate', *Journal of Personality and Social Psychology* 95(2)
(2008): 293–307.

Lucky colours and product evaluation: Thomas Kramer and Lauren
Block, 'Conscious and Nonconscious Components of Superstitious
Beliefs in Judgment and Decision Making', *Journal of Consumer
Research* 34(6) (2008): 783–93.

Lucky golf ball study and replication: Robert J. Calin-Jageman and
Tracy L. Caldwell, 'Replication of the Superstition and
Performance Study by Damisch, Stoberock, and Mussweiler
(2010)', *Social Psychology* 45(3) (2014): 239–45.

Paranormal belief and earnings: Shoko Yamane, Hiroyasu Yoneda,
and Yoshiro Tsutsui, 'Is Irrational Thinking Associated with Lower
Earnings and Happiness?', *Mind & Society*, no. 0123456789
(2019).

Astrology as a coping mechanism: Outi Lillqvist and Marjaana
Lindeman, 'Belief in Astrology as a Strategy for Self-Verification
and Coping with Negative Life-Events', *European Psychologist* 3(3)
(2004): 202–8.

Rituals: Alison Wood Brooks, Juliana Schroeder, Jane L. Risen,
Francesca Gino, Adam D. Galinsky, Michael I. Norton, and
Maurice E. Schweitzer, 'Don't Stop Believing: Rituals Improve
Performance by Decreasing Anxiety', *Organizational Behavior and
Human Decision Processes* 137 (2016): 71–85. The quoted ritual is
from p. 80.

Parents of child who died of meningitis: Meghan Grant, 'Parents'
Convictions in Son's Meningitis Death Upheld by Alberta Appeal
Court', CBCnews, 16 November 2017. <https://www.cbc.ca/news/
canada/calgary/david-collet-stephan-meningitis-death-son-failure-
provide-necessaries-appeal-1.4402665>.

Chapter 6: The future of superstition

MRI study: Li Lin Rao, Yu Zheng, Yuan Zhou, and Shu Li, 'Probing
the Neural Basis of Superstition', *Brain Topography* 27(6) (2014):
766–70.

Feng shui and corporate image: William Li Chang, 'Using Feng Shui
to Create a Positive Corporate Reputation', *Corporate Reputation
Review* 12(1) (2009): 43–51.

Casino loyalty: Daniel A. Guttentag and Mark E. Havitz, 'Superstition as a Personal Moderator in the Development of Commitment and Loyalty to and within Casinos', *Leisure/Loisir* 34(1) (2010): 1–25.

Superstitious slot machine: Bryan M. Kelly, Martin S. Lyons, Stephen E. Patton, and Daniel Savage, 'Superstitious Gesture Enhanced Gameplay System', US Patent 9,415,307, issued 16 August 2016.

Sports fan superstitions: Brendan Dwyer, Mark A. Slavich, and Jennifer L. Gellock, 'A Fan's Search for Meaning: Testing the Dimensionality of Sport Fan Superstition', *Sport Management Review* 21(5) (2018): 533–48.

Hong Kong hotel study: Stephen Pratt and Ksenia Kirillova, 'Are Hotel Guests Bothered by Unlucky Floor or Room Assignments?', *International Journal of Hospitality Management* 83 (June 2018): 83–94. Quote is from p. 92.

Ethics and consumer research: Stuart Vyse, 'Superstition, Ethics, and Transformative Consumer Research', *Journal of the Association for Consumer Research* 3(4) (2018): 582–90.

Risen on giving in to intuition: Jane L. Risen, 'Believing What We Do Not Believe: Acquiescence to Superstitious Beliefs and Other Powerful Intuitions', *Psychological Review* 123(2) (2016): 182–207.

Japanese study of paranormal belief: Shoko Yamane, Hiroyasu Yoneda, and Yoshiro Tsutsui, 'Is Irrational Thinking Associated with Lower Earnings and Happiness?' *Mind & Society*, no. 0123456789 (2019).

European Union survey of vaccine confidence: Heidi Larson, Alexandre de Figueiredo, Emilie Karafillakis, and Mahesh Rawal, 'The State of Vaccine Confidence in the EU: 2018', European Union (2018).

Gallup poll on global warming, 'Global Warming Concern Steady Despite Some Partisan Shifts.' Gallup.com. 28 March 2018. <https://news.gallup.com/poll/231530/global-warming-concern-steady-despite-partisan-shifts.aspx>.

Carl Sagan quote, Public Broadcasting Service, 'NOVA: Kidnapped by Aliens', 27 February 1996. Available at: <https://youtu.be/yr10Tt68Cu4>.

Further reading

Dictionaries and encyclopedias of superstitions

Rudi Brasch and Li Brasch, *How Did it Begin? The Origins of our Curious Customs and Superstitions* (MJF Books, 2006).

Brian Copenhaven (ed.), *The Book of Magic: From Antiquity to the Enlightenment* (Penguin Classics, 2017).

Harry Oliver, *Black Cats & Four-Leaf Clovers: The Origins of Old Wives' Tales and Superstitions in our Everyday Lives* (Penguin, 2010).

Iona Archibald Opie and Moira Tatem Opie (eds), *A Dictionary of Superstitions* (Oxford University Press, 1989).

Richard Webster, *The Encyclopedia of Superstitions* (Llewellyn Worldwide, 2012).

Chapter 1: The origins of superstition

Sarah Allan, *The Shape of the Turtle: Myth, Art, and Cosmos in Early China* (SUNY Press, 1991).

James Diggle (ed.), *Theophrastus: Characters: Cambridge Classical Texts and Commentaries*, revised edition, vol. 41 (Cambridge University Press, 2004).

Christopher A. Faraone and Dirk Obbink (eds), *Magika hiera: Ancient Greek Magic and Religion* (Oxford University Press on Demand, 1997).

John G. Gager (ed.), *Curse Tablets and Binding Spells from the Ancient World* (Oxford University Press, 1999).

Naomi Janowitz, *Magic in the Roman World: Pagans, Jews and Christians* (Routledge, 2002).

Dale B. Martin, *Inventing Superstition* (Harvard University Press, 2009).

Jon D. Mikalson, *Ancient Greek Religion* (John Wiley & Sons, 2009).

Solomon Alexander Nigosian, *The Zoroastrian Faith: Tradition and Modern Research* (McGill-Queen's Press-MQUP, 1993).

Daniel Ogden, *Magic, Witchcraft, and Ghosts in the Greek and Roman Worlds: A Sourcebook* (Oxford University Press, 2009).

Geraldine Pinch, *Egyptian Mythology: A Guide to the Gods, Goddesses, and Traditions of Ancient Egypt* (Oxford University Press, 2004).

Geraldine Pinch, *Magic in Ancient Egypt* (revised edition) (University of Texas Press, 2010).

James B. Rives, *Religion in the Roman Empire* (Wiley-Blackwell, 2006).

Richard Rutt, *The Book of Dhanges (Zhouyi): A Bronze Age Document Translated and with Introduction and Notes* (RoutledgeCurzon, 2002).

Hellmut Wilhelm (ed.), *The I Ching or Book of Changes* (Princeton University Press, 2011).

Chapter 2: Religious superstition

Michael David Bailey, *Magic and Superstition in Europe: A Concise History from Antiquity to the Present* (Rowman & Littlefield, 2007).

Karl Josef Heidecker, *The Divorce of Lothar II: Christian Marriage and Political Power in the Carolingian World* (Cornell University Press, 2010).

Charles Warren Hollister and Judith M. Bennett, *Medieval Europe: A Short History* (McGraw-Hill Humanities/Social Sciences/Languages, 2001).

Naomi Janowitz, *Magic in the Roman World: Pagans, Jews and Christians* (Routledge, 2002).

John Kelly, *The Great Mortality: An Intimate History of the Black Death, the Most Devastating Plague of All Time* (HarperCollins Publishers, 2005).

Roy Kotansky, *Greek Magical Amulets: The Inscribed Gold, Silver, Copper, and Bronze Lamellae: Part I. Published Texts of Known Provenance* (Springer-Verlag, 2014).

S. A. Smith and Alan Knight, *Religion of Fools? Superstition Past and Present*. Past & Present Suppl. 3 (Oxford University Press, 2008).

Chapter 3: The secularization of superstition

Anne Llewellyn Barstow, *Witchcraze: A New History of the European Witch Hunts* (Pandora, 1994).

Euan Cameron, *Enchanted Europe: Superstition, Reason, and Religion 1250–1750* (Oxford University Press, 2010).

Jason A. Josephson-Storm, *The Myth of Disenchantment: Magic, Modernity, and the Birth of the Human Sciences* (University of Chicago Press, 2017).

Christopher I. Lehrich, *The Language of Demons and Angels: Cornelius Agrippa's Occult Philosophia*, vol. 119 (Brill, 2003).

Brian P. Levack (ed.), *The Oxford Handbook of Witchcraft in Early Modern Europe and Colonial America* (Oxford University Press, 2013).

Helen Parish (ed.), *Superstition and Magic in Early Modern Europe* (Bloomsbury, 2015).

Steven Pinker, *The Better Angels of our Nature: A History of Violence and Humanity* (Penguin, 2011).

Keith Thomas, *Religion and the Decline of Magic: Studies in Popular Beliefs in Sixteenth and Seventeenth-Century England* (Penguin UK, 2003).

Chapter 4: Superstition in the modern world

Ann Braude, *Radical Spirits: Spiritualism and Women's Rights in Nineteenth-Century America* (Indiana University Press, 2001).

Clément Chéroux, Pierre Apraxine, Andreas Fischer, Denis Canguilhem, and Sophie Schmit, *The Perfect Medium: Photography and the Occult* (Yale University Press, 2005).

Arthur Conan Doyle, *The History of Spiritualism*, vol. 1 (The Psychic Bookshop, 1926).

Harry Houdini, *A Magician among the Spirits* (Cambridge University Press, 2011, originally published in 1924).

Krister Dylan Knapp, *William James: Psychical Research and the Challenge of Modernity* (University of North Carolina Press Books, 2017).

Nathaniel Lachenmeyer, *13: The Story of the World's Most Popular Superstition* (Thunder's Mouth Press, 2004).

Harry Whitaker, Christopher Upham, Murray Smith, and Stanley Finger (eds), *Brain, Mind and Medicine: Essays in Eighteenth-Century Neuroscience* (Springer Science & Business Media, 2007).

Chapter 5: The psychology of superstition

Bruce M. Hood, *The Science of Superstition: How the Developing Brain Creates Supernatural Beliefs* (Harper Collins, 2010).

Gustav Jahoda, *The Psychology of Superstition* (Aronson, 1974).

Bronislaw Malinowski, *Argonauts of the Western Pacific* (Routledge, 1922/2013).

Michael Shermer, *Why People Believe Weird Things: Pseudoscience, Superstition, and Other Confusions of our Time* (Macmillan, 2002).

Eugene Subbotsky, *Magic and the Mind: Mechanisms, Functions, and Development of Magical Thinking and Behavior* (Oxford University Press, 2010).

Stuart Vyse, *Believing in Magic: The Psychology of Superstition* (updated edition) (Oxford University Press, 2013).

Richard Wiseman, *The Luck Factor* (Arrow, 2004).

Chapter 6: The future of superstition

Tom Nichols, *The Death of Expertise: The Campaign Against Established Knowledge and Why it Matters* (Oxford University Press, 2017).

Paul A. Offit, *Deadly Choices: How the Anti-Vaccine Movement Threatens Us All* (Basic Books, 2015).

Steven Pinker, *Enlightenment Now: The Case for Reason, Science, Humanism, and Progress* (Penguin Books, 2019).

Index

For the benefit of digital users, indexed terms that span two pages (e.g., 52–53) may, on occasion, appear on only one of those pages.

Index

Index

CRITICAL THEORY
A Very Short Introduction
Stephen Eric Bronner

In its essence, Critical Theory is Western Marxist thought with
the emphasis moved from the liberation of the working class to
broader issues of individual agency. Critical Theory emerged
in the 1920s from the work of the Frankfurt School, the circle
of German-Jewish academics who sought to diagnose--and, if
at all possible, cure--the ills of society, particularly fascism
and capitalism. In this book, Stephen Eric Bronner provides
sketches of famous and less famous representatives of the
critical tradition (such as George Lukács and Ernst Bloch,
Theodor Adorno and Walter Benjamin, Herbert Marcuse and
Jurgen Habermas) as well as many of its seminal texts and
empirical investigations.

CHRISTIAN ETHICS
A Very Short Introduction
D. Stephen Long

This *Very Short Introduction* to Christian ethics introduces the topic by examining its sources and historical basis. D. Stephen Long presents a discussion of the relationship between Christian ethics, modern, and postmodern ethics, and explores practical issues including sex, money, and power. Long recognises the inherent difficulties in bringing together 'Christian' and 'ethics' but argues that this is an important task for both the Christian faith and for ethics. Arguing that Christian ethics are not a precise science, but the cultivation of practical wisdom from a range of sources, Long also discusses some of the failures of the Christian tradition, including the crusades, the conquest, slavery, inquisitions, and the Galileo affair.

www.oup.com/vsi

RELIGION IN AMERICA

A Very Short Introduction

Timothy Beal

Timothy Beal describes many aspects of religion in contemporary America that are typically ignored in other books on the subject, including religion in popular culture and counter-cultural groups; the growing phenomenon of "hybrid" religious identities, both individual and collective; the expanding numbers of new religious movements, or NRMs, in America; and interesting examples of "outsider religion." He also offers an engaging overview of the history of religion in America, from Native American traditions to the present day. Finally, Beal highlights the three major forces shaping the present and future of religion in America.

www.oup.com/vsi

CHAOS
A Very Short Introduction
Leonard Smith

Our growing understanding of Chaos Theory is having fascinating applications in the real world - from technology to global warming, politics, human behaviour, and even gambling on the stock market. Leonard Smith shows that we all have an intuitive understanding of chaotic systems. He uses accessible maths and physics (replacing complex equations with simple examples like pendulums, railway lines, and tossing coins) to explain the theory, and points to numerous examples in philosophy and literature (Edgar Allen Poe, Chang-Tzu, Arthur Conan Doyle) that illuminate the problems. The beauty of fractal patterns and their relation to chaos, as well as the history of chaos, and its uses in the real world and implications for the philosophy of science are all discussed in this *Very Short Introduction*.

'...Chaos...will give you the clearest (but not too painful idea) of the maths involved... There's a lot packed into this little book, and for such a technical exploration it's surprisingly readable and enjoyable - I really wanted to keep turning the pages. Smith also has some excellent words of wisdom about common misunderstandings of chaos theory...'

popularscience.co.uk

www.oup.com/vsi

WITCHCRAFT
A Very Short Introduction
Malcolm Gaskill

Witchcraft is a subject that fascinates us all, and everyone knows
what a witch is - or do they? From childhood most of us develop a
sense of the mysterious, malign person, usually an old woman.
Historically, too, we recognize witch-hunting as a feature of pre-
modern societies. But why do witches still feature so heavily in our
cultures and consciousness? From Halloween to superstitions,
and literary references such as Faust and even Harry Potter,
witches still feature heavily in our society. In this Very Short
Introduction Malcolm Gaskill challenges all of this, and argues
that what we think we know is, in fact, wrong.

'Each chapter in this small but perfectly-formed book could be the
jumping-off point for a year's stimulating reading. Buy it now.'

Fortean Times

CONSCIENCE
A VERY SHORT
INTRODUCTION

Paul Strohm

In the West conscience has been relied upon for two thousand years as a judgement that distinguishes right from wrong. It has effortlessly moved through every period division and timeline between the ancient, medieval, and modern. The Romans identified it, the early Christians appropriated it, and Reformation Protestants and loyal Catholics relied upon its advice and admonition. Today it is embraced with equal conviction by non-religious and religious alike. Considering its deep historical roots and exploring what it has meant to successive generations, Paul Strohm highlights why this particularly European concept deserves its reputation as 'one of the prouder Western contributions to human rights and human dignity throughout the world.

www.oup.com/vsi